The Bayonet

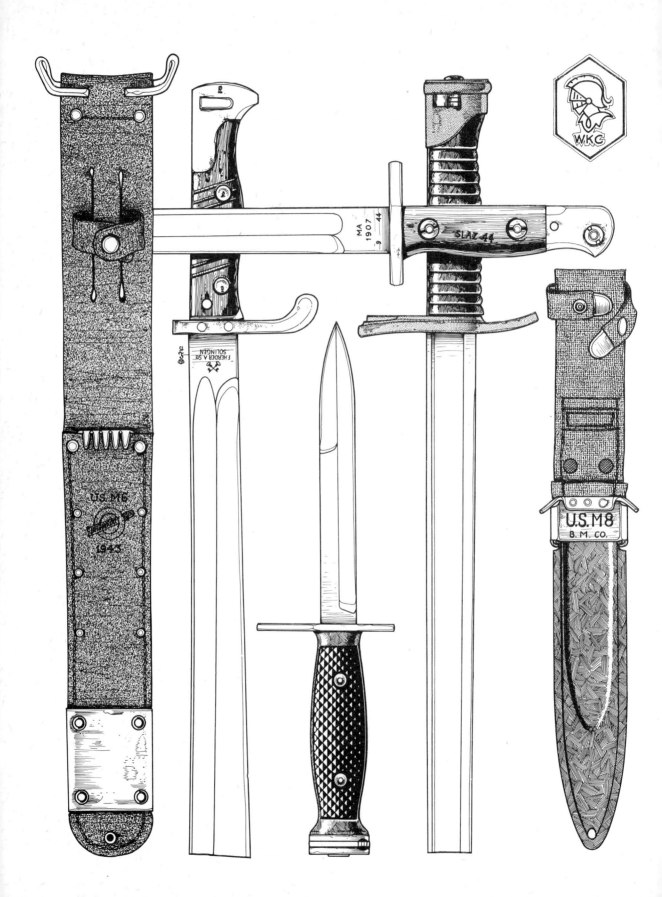

Anthony Carter
with contributions and illustrations by
John Walter

The Bayonet

A history of knife and sword
bayonets 1850-1970

Charles Scribner's Sons, New York

Printed in Great Britain
Library of Congress Catalog Card Number 74-5449
ISBN 0-684-13931-6

Contents and list of plates

The book consists of a series of consecutively-numbered articles, 1-60. The article number is keyed to the contents list, the illustrations and the illustration captions.

The system is best explained by an example, although there is really little to it. Article 31 refers to the Indian derivatives of the British Pattern 1907 sword bayonet, the so-called 'India Patterns'.

The country heading is self-explanatory and can be easily found: they are in alphabetical order. The relevant page and relevant illustrations then appear.

A glance at the contents list — which also serves the purpose of the index — gives the number of the article, a key to the weapons contained in the article, and a guide to whether or not there is an illustration.

5

Acknowledgements

Since I first began to write a regular column for *Guns Review* in 1965, many collectors have written with suggestions and corrections. Hence the response to each article, together with many requests to identify the weapons themselves, has provided additional information and corrected some statements that were found to be either untrue or half-truths. The result of the correspondence is this book, a much-revised and updated form of the original articles. It is hoped that most of the errors have been eliminated, for which much of the credit must go to the many readers of *Guns Review* who have always been so willing to help—and who have shared the information which has added to our knowledge of the bayonet.

I must first thank John Walter not only for his excellent illustrations—which are such an important part of this work—but also for his encouragement and advice; his attention to detail and knowledge of the subject have proved invaluable.

The section on German bayonets could not have been improved without the help and advice of Major aD Hans-Rudolf von Stein, who has continually shared his vast knowledge and allowed me to inspect his unequalled collection. Special thanks are also due to Colonel Clifford M Dodkins and to Dr James Maddox, who have both given freely of their time by allowing me to draw on their extensive collections for information while patiently answering my many questions.

Herb Woodend, of the Pattern Room at RSAF Enfield Lock, has been of great help in correcting many of the wrong designations previously accepted for British bayonets: I must thank him for his patience and continuous help.

The staffs of museums and archives have been of great help, and I would therefore like to express my gratitude to the following: Dr C H Roads and Ray Allen of the Imperial War Museum in London, William Reid and Michael Baldwin of the National Army Museum in London, Finn Askgaard of the Tøjhusmuseet in København (Copenhagen), Colonel Jacques Wemaere of the Musée de l'Armée in Paris, Captain A Gundeid of the Haermuseet in Oslo, and Mr K C B Görlitz of the Nederlands Leger en Wapenmuseum 'General Hoefer' at Leiden.

Many collectors have been of help in preparing this work and I do them all an injustice to list them below. My sincere thanks are however due to each, for without any one of them there would be a gap in this volume: Kevin Bestt, Homer Brett, Ray Brooker, Fred Datig, Ian Davidson, Frank Dupuis, Greg Engleman, Roger Evans, Chris Fox, Gordon Hughes, Michel Josserand, Ralph Karr, Dr John Kennaugh, Ted Millett, Ells Myers, Robert Platt, Guy Vaeremans, Peter White and William Yahn.

Finally I must thank Geoffrey Brown, editor of *Guns Review,* who first encouraged me to write the articles. I am extremely grateful to him for his advice and interest over the past ten years.

Anthony Carter, Loughton, 1974

The illustrations have, wherever possible, been drawn from weapons lent from the collections of Anthony Carter and Gordon Hughes—who each weathered persistent requests both to measure them and to describe their markings. In some instances, it was impossible to locate a weapon in time, and so the artwork was prepared from drawings, photographs, blueprints and verbal descriptions. I would therefore like to extend my thanks to the many people and to the organisations who generously supplied information from their files and collections. In addition to the people mentioned above, I would like to acknowledge the Musée d'Armes in Liége, the Schweizerisches Landesmuseum in Zurich, the Heeresgeschichtliches Museum in Wien, the Military Institue in Prahá (Prague), the Industrie- und Handelskammer zu Solingen, the Deutsches Klingenmuseum at Solingen-Gräfrath, Fabrique Nationale d'Armes de Guerre of Herstal-léz-Liége, and the staff of the Armouries and the Library of the Tower of London.

John Walter, Brighton, 1974

Introduction

The weapons in the hands of the armies of the mid-nineteenth century reflected the contemporary obsession with linear tactics and the advances in the development of contemporary firearms, whose progress in the two preceding centuries had—judged by what has since happened—been unspectacular.

Attempts were being made through the efforts of Delvigne, Tamisier, Minié and others to improve the quality of the basic infantrymen's firearms. This led to the adoption of expanding-ball ammunition, which occurred in most armies in the decade 1850-60, but the concept of the weapons from which it was fired differed little from that of those at Waterloo—single-shot firearms which could not be quickly loaded (especially when judged by the criteria of three decades later) and which were thus requiring of a means of secondary defence.

Hence the bayonet attained the status, at least so far as the first period with which this book is concerned, of an extension of the musket through which a pike could be provided; this could then prove useful in dissuading the enemy from pressing home a close-quarters attack with too much vigour, which was especially important on occasions when the second rank was in the middle of loading its weapons. It must be admitted that this was the theory: in practice the bayonet's morale value probably accounted for more than its practical utility!

By 1850, most nations concurred that the ideal length of the firearm/bayonet combination was about 2-2.25m, and that this was best achieved by issuing socket bayonets—with blades of triangular or quadrangular section for strength, achieved with minimum weight—with blades of between 500 and 600mm. This was, however, achieved at the cost of utility; socket bayonets were generally incapable of anything but a thrust.

At about the same time, some became convinced of the merits of the sword and sabre bayonets, many of which had been issued to specialised corps (especially riflemen) years previously. The Jäger, or riflemen, of Prussia had carried Hirschfänger weapons—literally 'deer's tooth', but colloquially a name for a huntsman's knife—since 1796, while comparable weapons had been issued in Austria as early as 1775. These had combined the functions of bayonet and short sword, and had done so to some useful purpose. In 1840 the French issued a sabre bayonet with a yataghan blade, in which a double curve was used, to riflemen and to noncommissioned officers. Although the life of the Mle 40 was short, owing to its replacement by the Mle 42 within two years, the craze for comparable bayonets began: many countries adopted similar designs in the period prior to 1870, many later examples of which were inspired by the appearance of the French Mle 66. Some, in fact, were no more than direct copies.

The advantages of sabre and sword bayonets—the former, by definition, with curved blades and the latter with straight ones—were important principally because the weapons were as useful off the firearm as they were on it. In some cases this was carried to extremes, and the British cutlass bayonets of the 1860s were good examples of patterns too unwieldy to be usefully used as such; they were, however, quite good hand-held swords. Another advantage, important in the mid-nineteenth century when each army was attempting to deck its troops in uniforms more resplendent than those of the others, was the garish appearance of many of the brass-hilted bayonets. Thus, in many cases, the bayonets came to be regarded as badges of élitism: the French Mle 42 and 42T, the Prussian Füsilier-Seitengewehr of 1860, the various riflemen's Hirschfänger, and the British Enfield sabre bayonets all came to be issued to troops who regarded themselves as superior to the line infantry. It was not until the French adoption of their Mle 66 that the cost of the sabre bayonets (one of the principal criticisms, along with excessive weight, often levelled at them) was regarded as insufficient to prevent their issue on a large scale.

In addition to the élite's decorative bayonets—which were, it must be admitted, much more impressive than the inconspicuous socket patterns then in general service—a second class of sabre bayonet, the tool-bayonet, also existed. In this the function of a special-purpose short sword (a pioneer's weapon for example) was combined with that of a bayonet, generally by adding a row of sawteeth to the blade back of a bayonet in which there was otherwise enough weight to facilitate use as an axe or a machète. In many cases the advantages were no more than illusory, and the weapons' utility as bayonets was usually close to none: some engineers' or pioneers' bayonets, for instance the Belgian Mle 68 and the Prussian models of 1869 and 1871, weighed considerably more than a kilogram . . .

At the outset, although as time progressed and sabre bayonets were lightened the delineation became less clear, the weapons were issued with carbines or short rifles (whose weight was generally about 500gm less than that of the infantry muskets) and were attached to muzzles on which were various auxiliary bars and tenons, designed to relieve the barrel of the stresses of a thrust applied only to a small specific point. This was again largely a pointless exercise and only complicated manufacture, so auxiliary tenons and bars were discarded towards the 1870s: the differences between the French Mle 66 and the Egyptian Remington bayonet of 1867 show this very clearly. Some nations, particularly the French (who remained keen on aberrant locking systems throughout the twentieth century as well) and the Italians, retained the tenons longer than others, but in general all such muzzle attachments had disappeared by the introduction in the late 1880s of the first generation of knife bayonets.

The principal wars of the era 1850-70—Crimea (1854-6), the US Civil War (1861-5), the Seven Weeks' War (1866) and the Franco-Prussian War (1870-71)—made very little impact on the bayonets, which were instead principally influenced by the advances in firearms design made at later date.

The bayonet designers of 1870 were obsessed by the idea of 'reach', and were generally determined to equip their troops with bayonets longer than those of their most likely opponents. By 1874 some, principally the French, had realised that in pursuit of such reach the sabre bayonets were becoming too heavy—hence the French Mle 74 épée bayonet ('Gras'), which used a strength-giving T-section blade to save weight when compared to its immediate predecessors. Belgium followed the French lead with their Garde Civique (Comblain) bayonet of 1882, while the Swedes and the Norwegians had used a similar concept on the long bayonet for the Jarmann rifle of 1880. The Jarmann bayonet actually had a blade of cruciform section, which was in turn taken by the French for their Mle 86 ('Lebel') épée bayonet; the Germans finally adopted a long slim pipeback blade—the ancestor of which was probably the British Lancaster Sappers' and Miners' Carbine bayonet of 1855—on their S98, but all ultimately realised that long thin blades were not really ideal.

The advent of smokeless powder and magazine rifles, which became large-scale issue at the end of the 1880s, changed the role of the bayonet and the tactics in which rifles and bayonets were used. It was no longer necessary, except in the cases of a few colonial wars where the native opponents were not usually aware of the potential firepower of the small-calibre magazine rifles, to provide a means of pike-defence for the troops. But then, if the pike was dead, what use was there for a bayonet at all? Many people asked the question and not all came to similar answers: some advocated the abolition of the bayonet completely, others (particularly in the USA) clung to the idea of the old rod bayonet long discarded in Europe, while others advocated combining the bayonet with such things as entrenching tools. Some measure of agreement was ultimately reached that it was necessary to provide the soldiers with some means of repulsing a close-quarters attack, even if the situation occurred only rarely, and that it would also be useful to incorporate in the bayonet some qualities of a general purpose knife. This was carried to its logical conclusion at a much later date—during World War 2—and the authorities of the 1880s and 1890s contented themselves with copying the German S71-84 knife bayonet, which had a blade of 250mm. Belgium, Britain, all Scandinavia, Austria-Hungary and others all changed to bayonets of this type: even the USA, where contemporary European developments sometimes passed unheeded, adopted a knife bayonet in 1892 for the Krag rifle.

Adoption of knife bayonets, 1884-1903

Germany[2]	1884	250mm blade
Austria-Hungary	1886/7	250mm blade
Japan[2]	1887	200mm blade
United Kingdom[2]	1888	305mm blade
Denmark[2]	1889	230mm blade
Switzerland	1889	300mm blade
Belgium[2]	1889	245mm blade
Italy	1891	300mm blade
USA[2]	1892	285mm blade
Romania	1892/3	250mm blade
Spain	1892/3	250mm blade
Norway[1]	1894	215mm blade
Sweden	1896	210mm blade
Serbia	1899	245mm blade
Greece[1]	1903	250mm blade

1. These countries also introduced sword bayonets at the same time.
2. These replaced or supplemented their knife bayonets at a later date with longer weapons, generally after the 'short rifle boom' of 1905-10.

The principal omissions from the list were France and Russia: the French clung to their épée bayonets, which caused the Germans to swing back to the old S71 (issued in all states except Bavaria with the Gew 88) and then to the S98: which was fair comment on the influence of the country they were most likely to fight. The Russians, alone amongst the armies, clung to the socket bayonet with something approaching fanaticism; a new socket bayonet was introduced in 1891, reintroduced with modifications in 1930, and influenced a whole generation of Soviet folding bayonets—even that on the Chinese-built Type 56 (AK) assault rifle.

Almost unseen by Europe, the Japanese reintroduced a sword bayonet in 1897, with a blade of 410mm and a single edge. The Japanese probably drew their inspiration from the French Mle 92 sword bayonet, and then themselves influenced many other nations owing to the results of the Russo-Japanese War (1904-5) in which military observers noted the Japanese using bayonet attacks at night. This more-or-less combined with the introduction in Britain of the Short Magazine Lee-Enfield rifle (SMLE) to provide an environment in which the countries who adopted short rifles also adopted longer bayonets to compensate for the reduction in reach. Thus the British took the Japanese 30th year bayonet of 1897 and produced from it the Sword Bayonet Pattern 1907, with a 432mm blade. The Americans, after yet another flirtation with the rod bayonet, had adopted a similar bayonet in 1905—when the Germans had also produced the S98-05, although issues did not begin on a large scale until 1908/9.

The onset of World War 1, and the resultant stagnated trenchscape, did much to prove the bayonet's uselessness in all but special sets of circumstances; the first thing to be discarded was the quillon on the crossguard, theoretically designed to catch an opponent's bayonet blade in combat (which could then be broken by a quick twist of the rifle), while the soldiers tended to use trench clubs and trench knives that proved beyond all doubt that the best blade length for a fighting/general purpose knife was in the region of 150mm. The long French épée bayonets broke with monotonous regularity, and the Germans readopted knife bayonets with blade lengths of 305mm and then 250mm. Various attempts, in most cases no more than the ideas of the lunatic fringe, were made to combine bayonets with wire cutters, but most mercifully failed to become practical realities: in any case, the wire entanglements became too thick and of too heavy a gauge of wire to be troubled by the puny bayonet-cutters. At the end of the war the old discussion over the bayonet's utility was revived, and there was again a good deal of speculation over the weapon's future.

An erroneous conclusion was formed by the military experts that the bayonet had been hardly used during the war. This assumption was based on the figures produced by field hospitals which stated (quite correctly) that they had treated very few bayonet wounds. The experts decided on this basis that the bayonet had seen little use, but they ignored the simple fact that while many soldiers were wounded by bullets, shells and bombs at a distance the bayonet was a *close* combat weapon; on occasions where assailants met with the bayonet, one usually received a fatal wound. The mortality figures would thus have told a very different story to the hospital reports. Wounds might have been rare; deaths were not.

The principal experimenters in this field were the British, alone amongst the other nations who clung to knife bayonets, and a series of trials held during the 1920s led to the introduction of the 'spike' bayonet (basically a modernised socket bayonet with a short cruciform blade) which could be easily produced and was designed purely for thrusting; the British board had considered that the Pattern 1907 bayonet was useless even as a means of chopping firewood and that it made little more than a useful poker. Hence, during World War 2, the British issued a series of spike bayonets with the No 4 rifle until they also finally agreed that the short general-purpose knife bayonet offered the most. This had been demonstrated by the Americans fighting in the Pacific Theater, who had first carried their M3 utility knife and then modified the design for use on the M1 carbine. The appearance of the Bayonet-Knife M4 merely confirmed the results of World War 1, at least so far as bayonet design was concerned, which had predicted the adoption of bayonets with double-edged blades some 150mm long and vestigial (but not totally absent) crossguards.

The Germans designed a knife bayonet—the now very rare S42—which contained various tools within the hilt, in the form of such things as bottle openers and screwdrivers, and the concept has since been further explored by the bayonet for the Armalite rifle of 1957 (which was a direct copy of the S42) and by such things as the NWM/Eickhorn development intended for the Stoner rifle and the Russian bayonet for the SVD sniper's rifle of 1967; the last two are both intended as wirecutters, in the sense of electrical wiring, and have insulated handles and scabbards which can be connected together to form a type of shears. Lightweight folding bayonets, particularly used by weapons emanating from Iron Curtain countries, are now also much favoured, but add a penalty in the form of weight—which is never so small as to be non existent—attached to the muzzle of the guns.

The future of the bayonet remains uncertain. Its detractors claim that in an age of mechanised warfare and automatic weapons, the bayonet has no part to play. But though the era of massed infantry attacks has probably departed forever, the role of the modern soldier encompasses more varied tasks than ever before. Civil strife has erupted throughout the world during the last decade and the army may find itself in a guerilla war, a policing action, guarding an airport or controlling crowds. Fixed bayonets have a greater psychological effect as a deterrent. A soldier will always have some need for a good general-purpose knife and its design can easily be incorporated in a bayonet.

Note

While revision of the articles was being undertaken, it was found that some were in real need of extensive alteration: it was also found that much of the published information on some parts of the subjects was either incomplete or simply wrong. This applied particularly to the British bayonets of the Snider and Martini-Henry era, where the principal reference books were discovered to be all but useless. In view of the extensive research necessary to correct two of the articles, it was thought preferable to delete them from this book. It would otherwise have been necessary to make unsubstantiated guesses or to repeat suspect material.

Research being undertaken on German ersatz bayonets, with a view to producing a reasoned catalogue of the various types, also influenced the revision. Owing to the differences between the draft catalogue and the articles that appeared in the 1966 *Guns Reviews,* the coverage of these bayonets has been drastically reduced.

The reduction of the material, in certain instances at least, has meant that new material could be added to cover some bayonets that were not previously mentioned. It has also been possible to increase the illustrative content to provide a better complement to the text.

Nomenclature

Wherever possible throughout the book, an attempt has been made to list the native terminology for the bayonets. Most of the terms used are self-explanatory — the French 'Baionnette' or the Italian 'Baionnetta' being but two — but there are others that are not so readily obvious. A list of the more confusing ones is given below.

Bodák (Czecholovakian): bayonet
Epée-baionnette (French): sword-bayonet, with a slim straight blade
Säbelbajonett (German, but generally used in Austria-Hungary): sabre bayonet
Sabre-baionnette (French): sabre-bayonet, with a curved blade
Sciabola-baionnetta (Italian): sword bayonet
Seitengewehr (German): literally 'sidearm', but used for a bayonet of virtually any pattern except socket
Shtik (Russian): bayonet
Yatagan or yataghan: a bayonet with a distinctive 'double-curved' or 'recurved' blade. This term is often used instead of 'sabre bayonet'

Blade
A   point
B   true edge
C   false edge
D   fuller
E   ricasso

Guard
F   crosspiece
G   muzzle ring
H   quillon
I   finial

Hilt
J   grips
K   flashguard
L   rivets or bolts
M   pommel
N   press stud

Knife bayonet

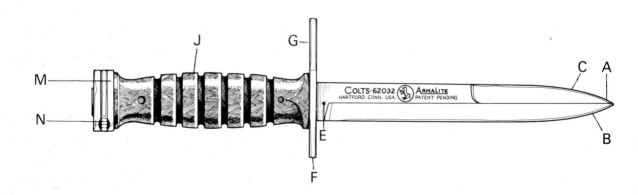

Sword bayonets

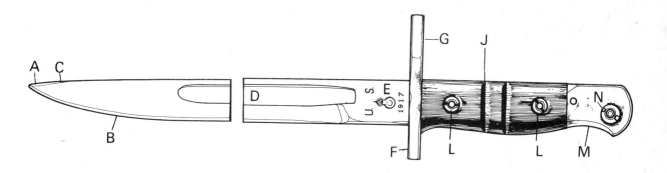

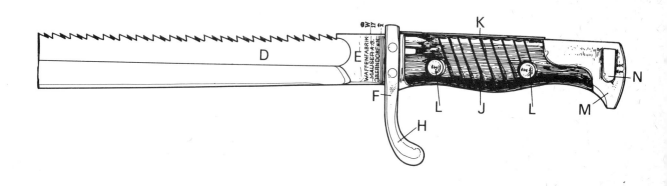

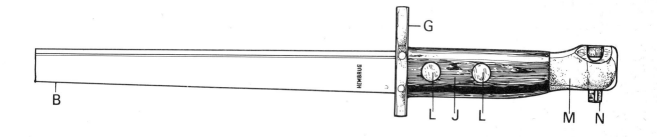

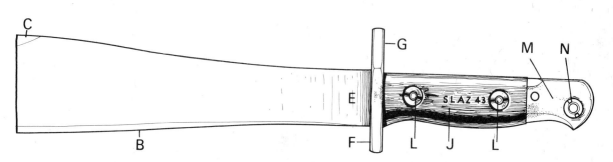

Sabre bayonet

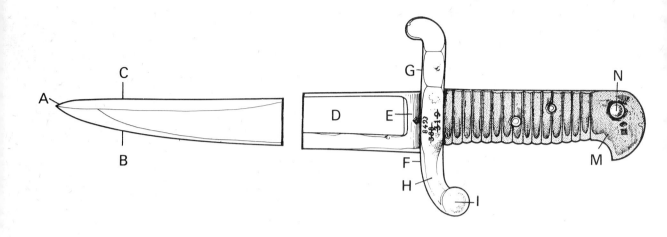

Scabbards

O   finial
P   chape
Q   body
R   topmount or locket
S   mouthpiece
T   frog
U   hilt loop

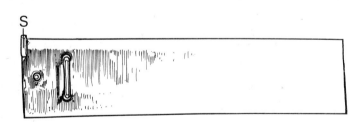

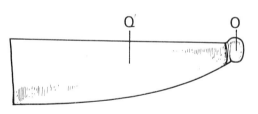

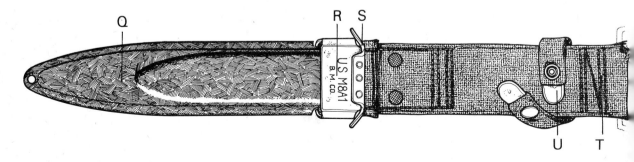

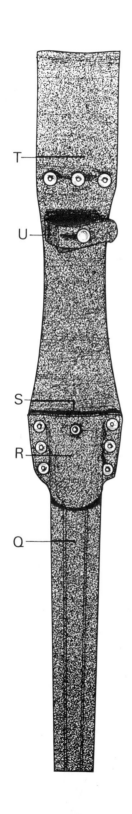

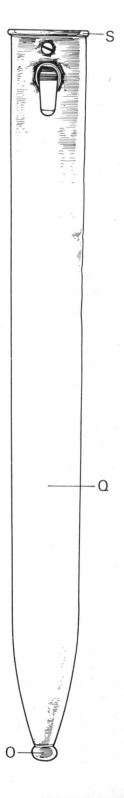

Australia

01. Machète and Owen machine carbine bayonets

Australia, like most other countries in the British Empire and Commonwealth, has usually used British arms to equip her troops. There have been exceptions—just as Canada briefly adopted the Ross rifle and the Indians manufactured the 'India Pattern' derivatives of the P07—two of which are the bayonets described here.

Australia, of course, was primarily involved in jungle warfare during World War 2 and there was thus a tendency to demand specialised weapons. In 1943 the machète bayonet was first manufactured for the Australians' shortened derivative of the Rifle No 1 Mk 3; the altered rifle was never adopted, but the bayonet (which in any case fitted the standard No 1 Mk 3 and Mk 3* rifles) was produced in small quantities. As its name implies, this bayonet has a broad machète or bolo blade, 289mm(11.38in) long and 50mm(2.00in) at its broadest. It is as heavily blued as the hilt, and has its lower edge sharpened for its whole length; the last 114mm(4.50in) of the back is also gradually sharpened to form a double-edged point. There are no fullers on the blade. The purpose of the design was to enable a soldier to clear jungle vegetation but its weight and shape were such that, after trials, it was never adopted. Like other combined machète/bayonets that had appeared previously it was too heavy and cumbersome for a bayonet, and not long enough to be an efficient machète.

The hilt is identical to that of the P07, without a quillon, and has an oiling hole drilled through the pommel. It is 122mm(4.81in) long, giving the bayonet an overall length of 411mm(16.19in). The scabbard is made of green canvas, stitched and reinforced by three copper rivets down the side. It has a steel mouthpiece and a webbing strap with a loop and a brass stud to hold the bayonet in the sheath and prevent swaying. A webbing frog is sewn to the back of the scabbard, which is 311mm(12.15in) long and 67mm(2.63in) wide.

The bayonets are usually to be found marked *SLAZ 43* on the wood grips after their manufacturers, Slazenger Sports Equipment Pty

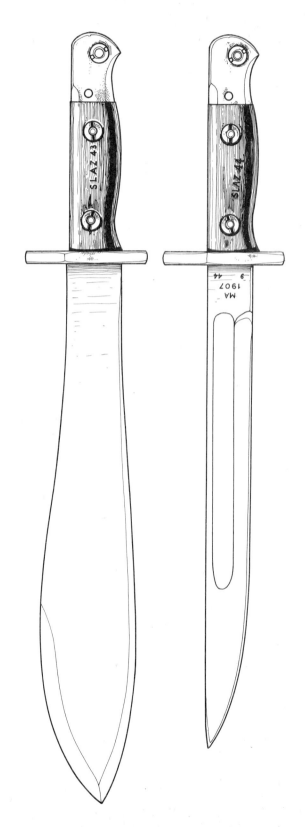

Ltd. A broad arrow is stamped on the blade. All evidence points to the fact that no more than 2000 of these bayonets were made, despite the presence of serial numbers that reach 5000.

The P43 machète was originally intended as a paratroop sidearm, for it was thought that its weight and blade form would be ideal to cut through tangled parachute lines.

1943 also saw the introduction of the short bayonet to fit the indigenous 9mm Owen machine carbine. This bayonet, at first no more than a shortened P07, was altered to use a newly-manufactured 254mm(10.00in) blade when it entered mass production. The result was the **Bayonet, Owen Machine Carbine, Pattern 1943,** which used a hilt identical to the P43 machète (and hence to the P07) that gave the weapon an overall length of 376mm (14.81in). The blade is single-edged with a point similar to that of the P07 where the cutting edge curves up to the back. It can easily be seen that the blade is not a shortened full-length type by the fullers, which are no more than 140mm(5.50in) long and which end 85mm(3.63in) from the point.

The scabbard is of leather with steel mounts of the same design as the British No 1 Mk 2; the topmount ends in a straight edge whereas the chape is curved where it meets the leather body. The frog-stud is round and the overall length of the scabbard is 292mm(11.50in).

The Owen bayonet remained in service with the Australian Army until the late 1960s, although none had been manufactured for many years; the blades are stamped *MA 1907* (MA being Munitions Australia, and 1907 the pattern stamp) above the actual date of manufacture: *eg* 11 44 for November 1944. The blades also bear the broad arrow and the mark *OA* for the Orange Arsenal.

The Owen machine carbine has now been replaced in the Australian Army by the 9mm Submachine-gun F1, which uses the native-made L1A3 bayonet.

Austria-Hungary

02. Sabre bayonets, 1867–1886

After the disastrous Austrian participation in the Seven Weeks' War of 1866, when their armies were signally defeated by those of Prussia and her allies, the Austrian ordnance carried out trials to find a suitable breechloading rifle for the troops: the result was the *Infanterie- und Jägergewehr system Werndl-Holub Modell 1867*, which was introduced on 28th July 1867 together with the **Säbelbajonett Modell 1867.**

The M67 has a yataghan blade, 580mm(22.83in) long, which is fullered on both sides. The steel hilt has chequered black leather grips, retained on one side by four rivets and on the other by three rivets and the screw of the leaf spring. The pommel contains the T-slot while the end of the press-stud—which protrudes from the left or reverse side of the hilt—is capped by a large steel button.

The crossguard has a swept forward quillon and the muzzle ring, close to the hilt and with a diameter of 18.5mm(0.728in), is surmounted by a ball finial.

In 1870 a modified version of the M67, the **Säbelbajonett Modell 1870,** was introduced in which the blade (although of the same length) had been lightened by deepening the fullers and by making it appreciably slimmer. The M70 has a stepped-back muzzle ring and the old ball finial is replaced by an adjusting screw, with which the diameter of the ring can be varied to fit the barrels of rifles whose manufacturing tolerances were excessive. The M70 is otherwise similar to the M67.

Shortened versions of both were later officially sanctioned, perhaps c.1877/80, in which the blades were cut to 470mm(18.50in) and refinished by base workshops. These show none of the clumsy alterations usually associated with shortened bayonets, and some sabre bayonets can also be found with bushed muzzle rings—probably for some of the later Mannlicher rifles, or for some of the obsolete

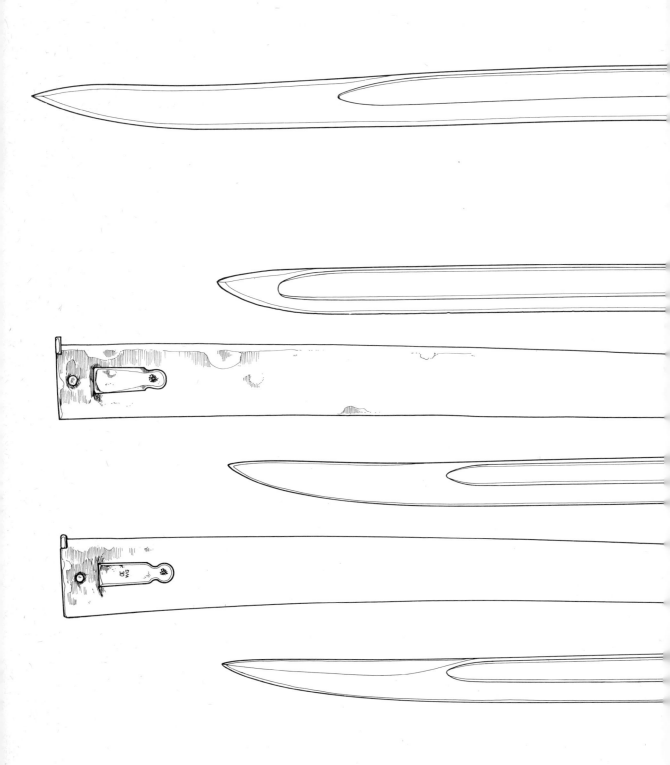

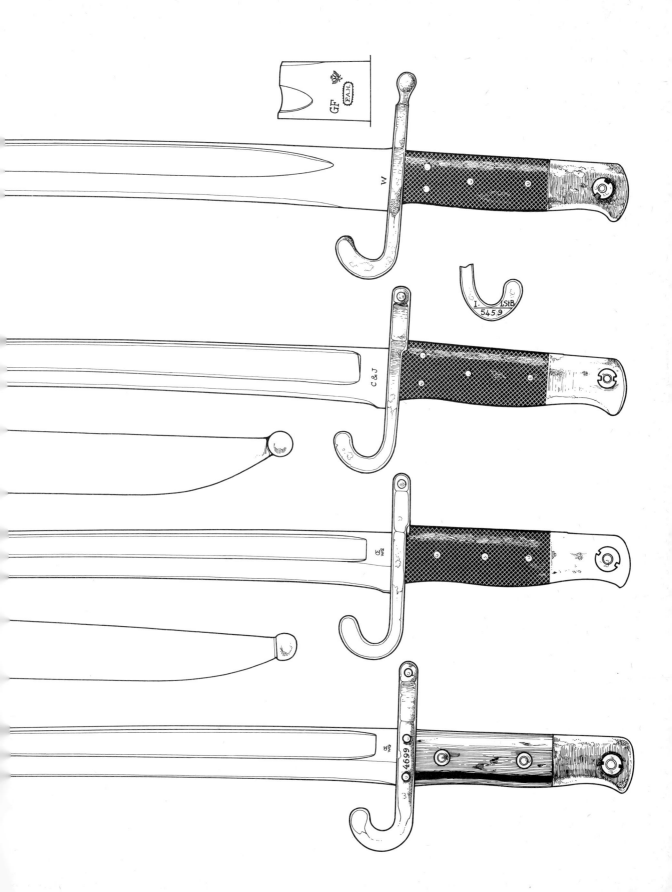

German rifles used during World War 1 by some Austro-Hungarian troops.

The scabbards for the M67 and M70 sabre bayonets are all-steel types with frog-studs and with the blade-retaining springs riveted inside the mouthpiece. These were also officially shortened from 615mm(24.21in) to 505mm(19.88in).

The third sabre bayonet, the **Säbelbajonett Modell 1873**, was introduced on 10th February 1874 to accompany the modified Infanterie- und Jägergewehr of the 1873, whose introduction was also slightly delayed. The M73 is similar to the earlier weapons, but was manufactured with a blade of only 465mm(18.31in) which is deeply fullered. The steel guard has a forward swept quillon, the muzzle ring is topped by an adjusting screw, and the chequered leather grips are retained by three steel rivets in a line. The press-stud assembly is unusual in that the spring is an external coil type, trapped between the head of the stud and the pommel-side in unique fashion. All M73 bayonets produced after 1881 were fitted with wood grips retained by two large rivets, while some earlier weapons repaired after that date were also regripped.

The M73 scabbard, painted black in peacetime but field grey in war, is again of steel and is approximately 485mm(19.09in) long.

All three types may be found with an NCO's knot loop at the pommel, attached by a screw (original factory-made NCO's bayonets) or by a simple stout wire bent into a hole drilled through the pommel-beak. It is thought that each of the latter pattern signifies that its owner was promoted in the field, whereupon the loop was added.

The majority of the sabre bayonets were made at Steyr by Österreichische Waffenfabrik-Gesellschaft, but some of M67 type are known to have been made in Solingen (by Alexander Coppel & Cie and by Clemen & Jung) and still others bear names of small Austrian firms.

A fourth pattern of sabre bayonet, the **Säbelbajonett Modell 1886**, seems to have been produced prior to the adoption of the knife bayonets. This weapon utilises a M73 blade with a hilt similar to that of the Austrian-made Portuguese M86 sword bayonet, and it is thought that less than 10000 were made. The muzzle ring has a diameter of 17.5mm(0.689in).

03.   Knife bayonets, 1886–1888

The 1880s saw the Austro-Hungarian ordnance experimenting with the rifle designs of Ferdinand von Mannlicher, and the result was the introduction on 20th June 1886 of the Infanterie Repetier-Gewehr Modell 1886—a bolt-action rifle firing an 11.15mm calibre cartridge that used a charge of black powder. The opportunity was also taken to devise a short knife bayonet of the type then being introduced to the German armies, and this consequently led to the appearance (c.1887) of the **Bajonett Modell 1886**. This is now rare, since only 93000 M86 rifles were manufactured before the introduction of the 8mm M88 rifle two years later; the small-calibre rifle was accompanied by the **Bajonett Modell 1888**, which differed from its predecessor principally in the reduced diameter of the muzzle ring.

The bayonets are however similar, and so one description suffices for both; the single-edged knife blades, officially 250mm(9.84in) long but subject to considerable manufacturing tolerances, are deeply fullered and the cutting edge faces downwards in conventional manner—quite unlike the blade of the later M95, which is reversed. The steel guard has a muzzle ring with a diameter of either 17.5mm(0.689in) for the M86 or 16.5mm(0.650in) for the M88, and NCOs' bayonets have quillons and knot loops. The muzzle ring is topped by an adjustable ring, although some M88 bayonets

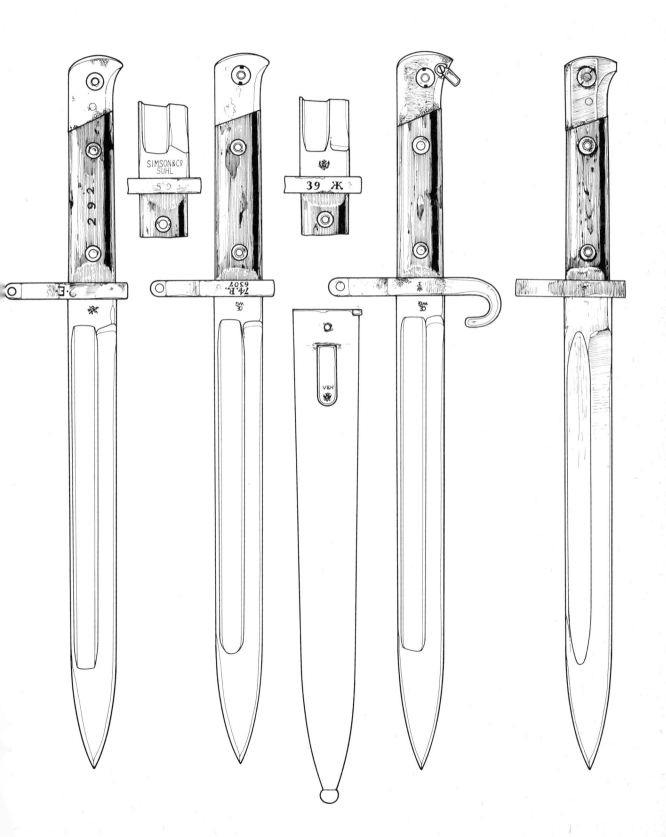

produced in World War 1 lack this feature and instead have a solid ring.

The distinctive NCOs' weapons were produced in many forms: some have proper arsenal-made knot loops, while others utilise simple pieces of heavy-gauge wire. On some M88 bayonets quillons have been added by brazing extensions to otherwise quillonless guards.

The scabbards of all are of steel, black in peace and field-grey in war, with ball ferrules and blade retaining springs held by rivets; the frog stud is 32mm(1.25in) long and rounded at the end.

The bayonets were made in Austria by Österreichische Waffenfabrik-Gesellschaft of Steyr (mark OE over WG) and in Hungary by Fémáru Fegyver és Gépgyár of Budapest (mark FG over GY); others were made in Germany—the names of E & F Hörster & Cie and Alexander Coppel & Cie, both of Solingen, have been noted—while still more bear the names of other Austrian companies. Many of the scabbards seem to have been made by Vogel & Nott, of Hartberg in Styria, whose mark was V & N.

In addition to the Austro-Hungarian bayonets, the M88 was also used in Bulgaria, whose weapons are distinguished by the cypher 'crown F' on the guard.

04.   Knife bayonet, 1895

Fault had been found with the actions of the M86 and M88 rifles, and so in 1890 the Austro-Hungarians introduced a Mannlicher-designed cavalry carbine in which an improved bolt system was used: The gun, which was not initially fitted with a bayonet, proved successful and was followed by the series of 1895 which contained an infantry rifle, a cavalry carbine and a short rifle (Stutzen) for the engineers and the artillery.

The **Bajonett Modell 1895** has a short single-edged blade of 250mm(9.84in), each side of which bears a fuller, but the cutting edge is upwards—the opposite of standard practice, although it was continued in postwar years by the Czechs. The crossguard is riveted to the tang, the wood grips are retained by two rivets set in washers, and the steel pommel contains an internal coil-spring press-stud mechanism. The diameter of the muzzle ring of all the service bayonets was 15.5mm(0.610in). A T-groove was used to attach the bayonet to the rifle's lug placed under the nosecap, which meant that the bayonet did not fix in a horizontal plane like the M86 and M88.

A second bayonet, the **Bajonett Modell 1895 für Stutzen und Karabiner**, was also issued. This was first designed for the short rifle, to be issued to engineers and artillery, but was later adopted for the second pattern of M95 cavalry carbine: the first experimental M95 carbine was not fitted for a bayonet. The only difference between the two type of M95 bayonet lay in the addition to the Stutzen pattern of an auxiliary foresight on top of the muzzle ring, for it had been found that the firing with fixed bayonet altered the point of bullet impact by interfering with the vibrations set up in the barrel. Most Stutzen bayonets have laterally-adjustable sights, but some were converted in World War 1 from standard bayonets by riveting a small conical block to the ring; others were made after c.1915 with the conical sight, but in these cases the block and the crossguard are integral parts of each other.

Both patterns of bayonet also exist in a multitude of NCOs' types—some with loops attached by screws, others with pieces of wire bent into pommel holes, still others with new quillons (either brazed to the existing guard or separate components sliding over the blade), while versions with plated blades were also made for 'dress' and off-duty wear.

The M95 scabbards are of steel, each tipped by a round ferrule and possessing a frog-stud, while the blade retaining springs are riveted in place. The scabbards were painted black in peacetime and field-grey in times of war.

The bayonets were made by Österreichische Waffenfabrik-Gesellschaft (OE over WG) and by Femáru Fegyver és Gépgyár (FG over GY), while many of the scabbards were made by Vogel & Nott. FGGY bayonets have noticeably-squarer fullers than the OEWG products. Austro-Hungarian bayonets generally bear the displayed eagle mark on the ricasso. Some, however, may be found marked ČSZ on the blade, which signifies Czech issue, and others bear Bulgaria's 'crown F' cypher on the guard.

18   Bajonett M95, bearing postwar Czech markings
19   Obverse ricasso and guard of 18
20   Scabbard M95, with Czech marks on the frog-stud
21   Bajonett M95, NCO's converted pattern, made by OEWG and with interesting blade etching
22   Bajonett M95, NCO's pattern, for Stutzen M95; with alternative patterns types of sight
23   Bajonett M88/95, a hybrid made for the M88 rifle; FGGY make, probably post-1918

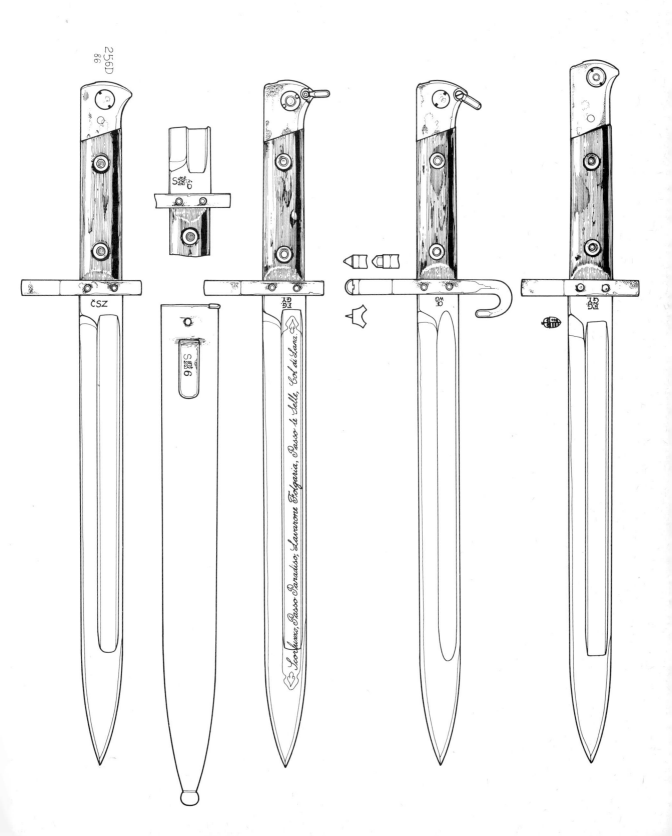

Belgium

05. Sabre and sword bayonets, 1868–1882

These bayonets owe their design to French weapons that had passed before: the Mle 68 is a copy of the French Mle 66 'Chassepot' sabre bayonet, while the Mle 82 draws heavily upon the design of the French Mle 74 épée bayonet intended for the Gras rifle. Belgium continued to look for influence to France even after the Franco-Prussian war of 1870/1, and it was not until the adoption in 1889 of a Mauser-designed rifle that the focus changed.

The Mle 68 bayonet, correctly called the **Yatagan de la Carabine, Modèle 1868**, has a recurved blade some 570mm(22.5in) long, in the French style and deeply fullered. The hilt has fifteen ribs and its back has the long groove and chamfered edges found on the French Mle 66. The principal differences between the Belgian and French weapons are the former's more rounded pommel and the fact that the Belgian weapon's leaf spring is retained by a screw rather than by a rivet. The rivet through the hilt, the purpose of which is to secure the blade, is ground flush with the brass only on Belgian Mle 68 bayonets.

The guard has a swept forward qullon that ends in a ball finial and the muzzle ring is topped by an adjusting screw by which the diameter can be varied. According to Belgian records the original scabbard was of black cowhide with brass mounts, but most examples now seen of the Mle 68 are found in all-steel scabbards of French type—complete with frog loop.

The Mle 68 was issued with the Carabine Mle 68 ('Albini'), which although known as a 'carbine' was really more a short rifle issued to riflemen and others. Some firearms of the Mle 89 series are described in Belgian records as *avec yatagan*, but this does not mean the Mle 68 sabre bayonet. The Carabine Comblain Mle 71, another short rifle and not to be confused with the Comblain cavalry 'Mousqueton' of the same year, also seems to have used the Mle 68 bayonet.

The Mle 82, **the Épée-Baionnette pour le Fusil Comblain des Corps spéciaux de Garde Civique, Modèle 1882**, is not such a direct copy of of its its French predecessor in that both the hilt and

scabbard are different. It has a T-section blade identical to that of the French Mle 74, 520mm(20.50in) long, while the hilt has wood grips and a steel pommel. The back of the hilt is flat and the T-groove for the rifle's attachment bar is a mere 28mm(1.12in) long. The leaf spring is held by a screw, and the grips by rivets. The steel guard has a swept forward quillon and a plain muzzle ring without an adjusting screw, while the steel scabbard—which tapers to a ball ferrule—differs from that of the French Mle 74 in that it has a frog-stud rather than a frog loop.

Many of the Comblain bayonets were seized in 1914 by the Germans; some were thereafter rehilted, although others were simply modified by removing the muzzle ring and changing the press-stud from the reverse side of the hilt to the obverse or right side. As some French Mle 74 bayonets were also rehilted, the differences can only be told by the markings on the blades.

A variation of the Mle 82 was issued as a sidearm to bandsmen, in which the muzzle ring was solid and where there was neither press-stud nor attachment groove. The flat back of the pommel was stamped with a lyre.

06. Engineers' bayonets, 1868–1880

Belgium's engineer bayonets combine French and German influence in their design; the hilts are very similar to those of the French Mle 66 sabre bayonets, while the saw-backed blades are distinctively Germanic. In fact many of the weapons, particularly specimens of the earlier Mle 68, were made in Solingen by firms such as Alexander Coppel & Cie.

The Mle 68—the **Yatagan-scie de la Carabine, Modèle 1868**—has a solid brass hilt with fifteen ribs and with the hilt-back slotted and chamfered in the French style. The leaf spring is retained by a screw and the tang-retaining rivet is ground flush with the hilt, while so is the blade tang which would otherwise protrude at the pommel. The guard has a swept forward quillon with an adjusting screw on top of the ring. The blade is 485mm(19.00in) long and 38mm(1.50in) wide, with deep wide fullers and a sawback containing 38 double teeth. The scabbard is of black leather with brass mounts and a frog loop.

The Mle 80 (**Yatagan-scie Modèle 1880**), issued with Comblain or Albini short rifles, has a similar hilt to its predecessor but with seventeen ridges. The blade is slimmer and shorter, measuring 465mm(18.25in) overall and only 30mm(1.18in) wide. The sawback has 31 double teeth, and the muzzle ring diameter is approximately 17-17.5mm(0.669-0.689in)—the same as that of the two Mle 68 bayonets. The scabbard is again of brass-mounted leather and retains the frog loop.

Both these engineers' bayonets are rare and are of especial interest in that they were the only sawbacked models adopted by the Belgian forces—while the French, whose influence in Belgium was important, never used comparable types.

Belgian bayonet markings

Some of the markings on these bayonets are especially useful, particularly as Belgian weapons (like those of France) are often covered in inspection marks. On the obverse, or right side, of the blade is the date of manufacture; the mark *GB* within an oval, usually found on the reverse ricasso, signifies *Gouvernement Belge*—the official property stamp—while various poinçons de contrôle (inspection marks) appear elsewhere. Some of these are in the form of letters surmounted by the Belgian lion statant. Occasionally the bayonets can be found bearing the trademark of their manufacturers—generally Alexander Coppel & Cie of Solingen if made in Germany—but many were produced in Liège and bear no distinctive marks.

07. Knife and sword bayonets, 1889

The Belgian war department adopted their Mauser rifle, officially known as the *Fusil à répétition, Système Mauser, Modèle 1889*, in October 1889, although the first production rifle was not delivered until 6th February 1892. The opportunity was also taken to devise a series of bayonets, each of which made use of a common hilt.

Two patterns were issued to the regular army, one with a knife blade of 250mm(9.84in) and the other with a long sword blade of 550mm(21.65in); the blade of the sword bayonet was slightly narrower than that of the knife type (23mm/0.91in compared to 26mm/1.02in) to save a little weight. The hilts were identical, with wood grips retained by rivets set in washers and steel pommels bearing standard internal coil-spring press-studs. Each bayonet had a steel guard with a swept forward quillon ending in a flattened ball finial, and each possessed a muzzle ring whose diameter was 17.5mm(0.689in).

The knife bayonet, the **Baionnette du Fusil Mauser Mle 89**, was issued from 21st March 1892 to the line infantry with the standard Mle 89 rifle. The sword bayonet was issued from 9th May 1904 with the firearms described as *avec yatagan*—the Carabine pour Gendarmerie à pied et Artillerie de fortresse Mle 89 (*i.e.* for dismounted police and fortress artillery units) and the Carabine Allégée de Gendarmerie à Cheval Mle 89. Both bayonets were issued with steel scabbards, the shorter model having a rectangular frog-stud and the longer type an oval one.

A variation of the long model was issued as a musician's sidearm, in which case the weapon had no means of attaching it to the gun and also possessed a solid muzzle ring. The pommels of such weapons are usually found stamped with a lyre.

In addition to the bayonets of the regular army, another pattern was issued from 11th February 1896 to the Garde Civique (civil guard). This has a blade of 300mm(11.81in), but quite why this was thought necessary is a mystery. The Garde Civique's cyclists carried a version of the same bayonet with a smaller muzzle ring, which fitted a special carbine with a different muzzle to the standard Mle 89; the ring diameter of this pattern was 15mm(0.591in) compared to 17.5mm(0.689in) of all the regular models.

Some Mle 89 bayonets may be found with their muzzle rings removed to fit the German Gewehr 88; these, and other unaltered bayonets marked *Deutsch* or *Deutschland* on the pommels, were seized during World War 1 by the Germans.

24   Sabre-Baionnette Mle 68, number R1204, 1869; probably made by P J Malherbé & Cie of Liège
25   Obverse hilt and ricasso
26   Topmount, scabbard Mle 68
27   Épée-Baionnette Mle 82, number 29784
28   Obverse hilt and guard
29   Mle 82 musician's sidearm, lyre-stamp on hilt-back
30   Scabbard Mle 82
31   Épée-Baionnette Mle 82, number 13178, modified by Germany c.1915
32   Obverse hilt showing modified press-stud
33   Yatagan-scie Mle 68
34   Yatagan-scie Mle 80, by Alexander Coppel & Cie of Solingen, 1888: number V4603
35   Obverse hilt and ricasso
36   Scabbard Mle 80

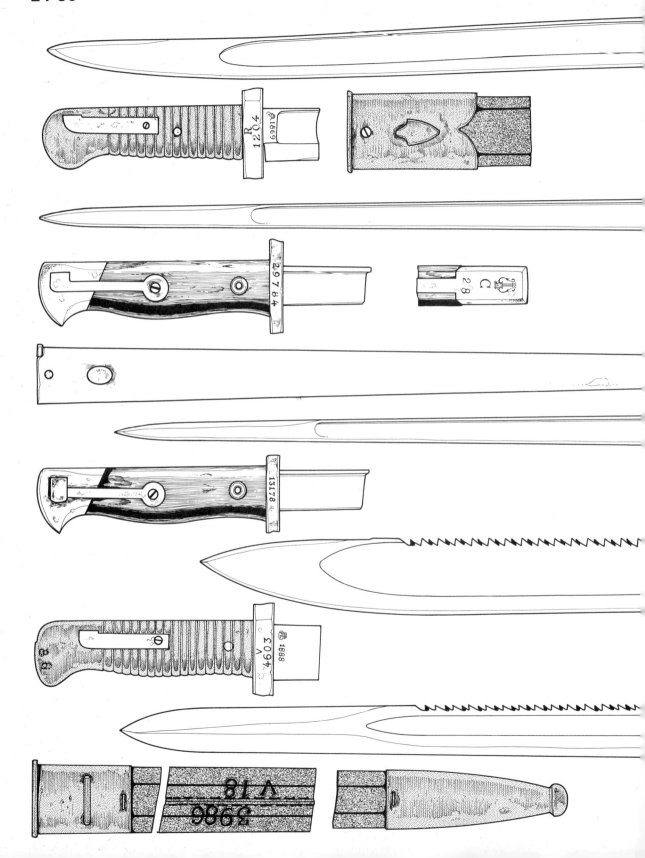

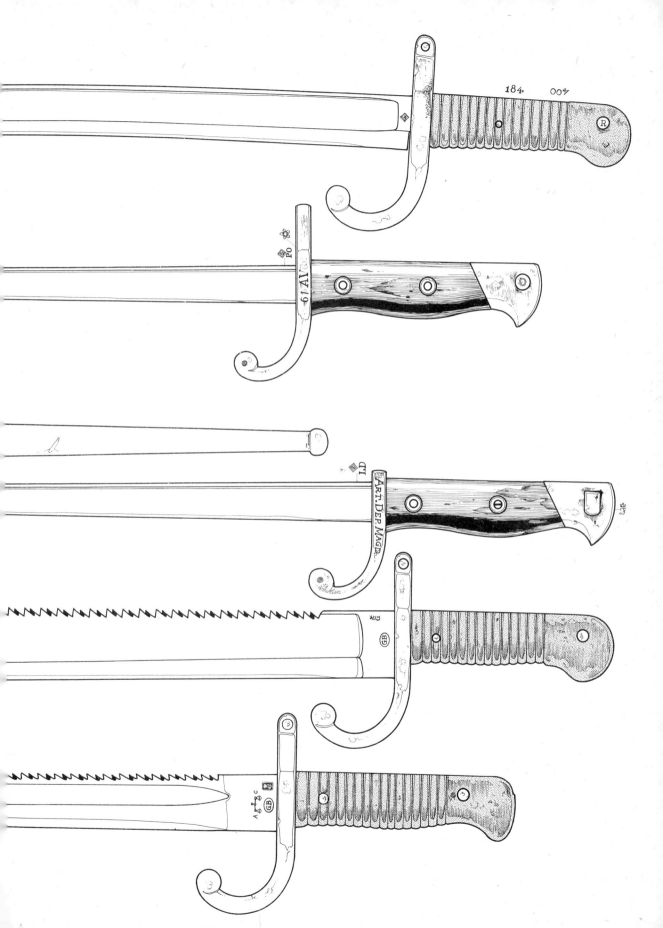

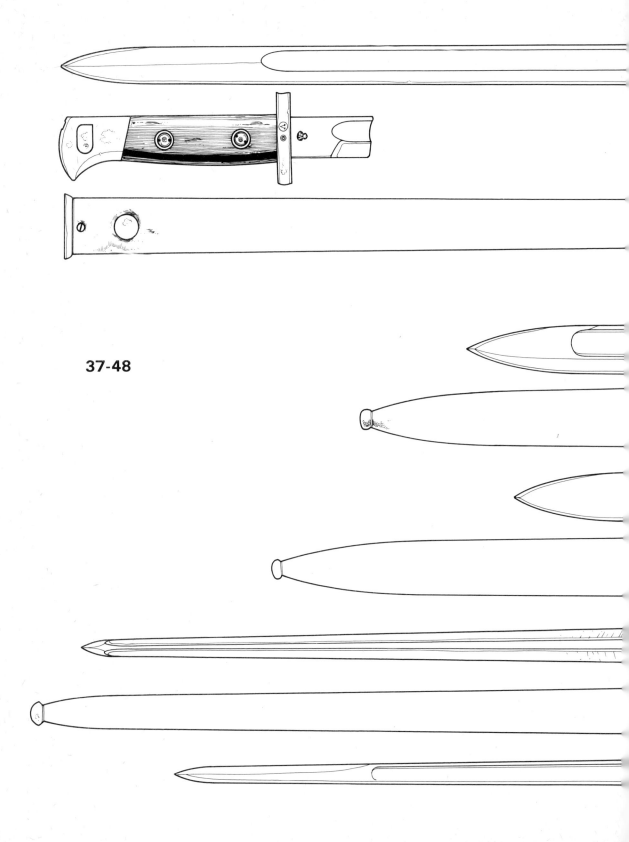

37-48

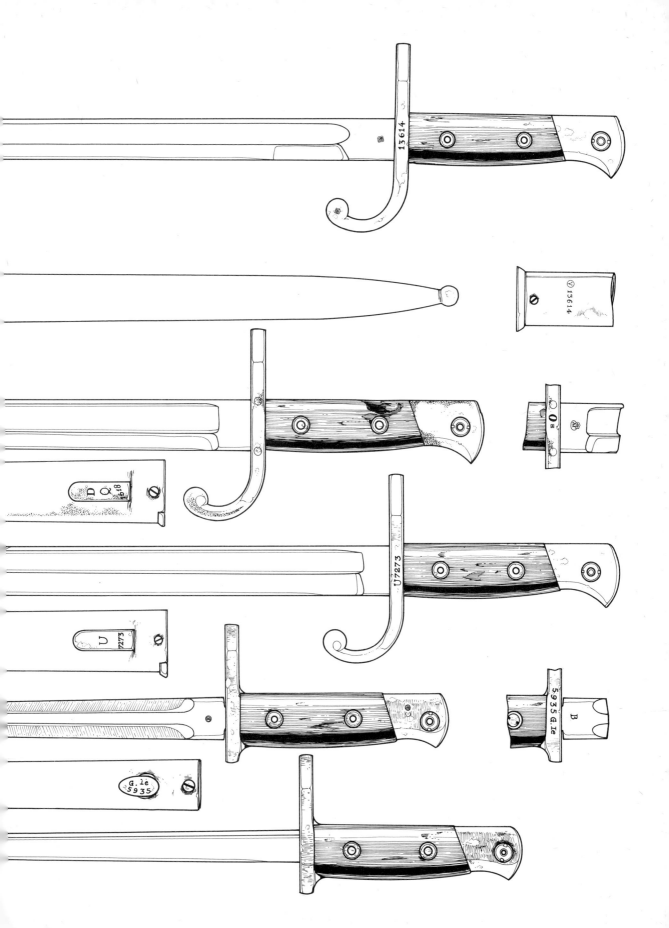

A further Mle 89-type bayonet, with a conventional full-size muzzle ring and a 250mm blade, is known in which the blade is reversed so that the edge is upwards. The single specimen examined bore the serial number *E 1354* and was marked on both the crossguard and the frog-stud with the letter *P*. Whether or not the P represents 'Prototype' is speculation, but it is suggested that this particular bayonet was one of a batch made between February and March of 1892 for trials that led to the standard Mle 89.

08.   Sword bayonets, 1916–1935

The Belgian bayonets of the immediate postwar period have been definitely identified for a long time, so far as collectors have been concerned; now, however, there is reason to revise the terminology.

Prior to World War 1, Fabrique Nationale had been producing a bayonet for the Mle 89 rifle and—according to the manufacturers at least—this bayonet was adopted in small numbers by the Belgian army just prior to the war with the intention of ultimately replacing the motley collection of knife bayonets then in service. The bayonet is distinguished by a longer blade than any of the Mle 89 series, some 330mm(12.99in), and a different hilt with shaped grips and the press-stud moved to the obverse or right side. Most surviving specimens of this bayonet have muzzle rings of 15.0mm(0.591in), which suggests that they were fitted to rifles in which the barrel jacket was either absent or in which the bayonet bar was moved forward by about 6mm(0.25in). The Belgians are reputed to have introduced a Mle 16 rifle during the war, and it may be that this rifle—like the Garde Civique cyclist's carbine—had a modified muzzle. In 1924 the authorities adopted another bayonet, the **Épee-Baionnette Modèle 1924,** which was designed to replace those weapons then in service. The bayonet, listed by FN as the 'baionnette Spéciale Belge et coloniel, 1924', has a steel hilt with wood grips of typically-Belgian shape. The steel pommel contains a T-slot and a conventional internal coil-spring

press-stud protruding from the left or reverse side of the hilt, while it meets the grips diagonally. The 450mm(17.72in) blade is double-edged for its entire length and the edges are milled out to leave a raised medial rib; the finish of the blade is poor and there are usually noticeable grinding marks. The scabbard is of steel and tapers to a ball ferrule; both the scabbard and the bayonet are heavily blued. Two types of Mle 24 bayonet exist, differing only in the diameter of the muzzle ring: those with 17.5mm(0.689in) rings fit the various Mle 89 rifles and carbines using the original Mle 89 bayonets, while the Mle 24 bayonets with rings of 15mm(0.591in) fit the Garde Civique Cyclistes' carbine, the Mle 16 rifle, and the later Mle 35 and Mle 36 rifles. It will be noted that the designation 'Modèle 1916' for the large-ring Mle 24 is now apparently discredited.

There is, however, a second bayonet with a hilt similar to that of the Mle 24. This, the **Épée-Baionnette de la Carabine de Gendarmerie á pied et à cheval, Mle 16,** was issued to the police formations to replace the long Mle 89 sword bayonet. It is this bayonet, it is thought, that has led to the designations 'Mle 16' and 'Mle 24' being applied to the two versions of the Mle 24 bayonet. The Mle 16 Gendarmerie bayonet is fitted with the T-section blade of the old Mle 82 (Comblain) Garde Civique épée pattern, shortened to about 450mm(17.72in).

The two types of bayonet, Mle 16 and Mle 24, are strong in spite of their slender blades: the old T-section blade was well-proven, and gained strength by shortening, while the medial-ribbed Mle 24 type had also been used on such bayonets as the British P88 and P03. Both the Belgian types, however, were principally designed as thrusting weapons and have no real cutting edges.

37   Sabre-Baionnette Mle 89, number V13614, made by Jules Ancion et Cie of Liège
38   Obverse hilt and ricasso of 37
39   Scabbard, long, Mle 89
40   Scabbard, long, Mle 89; top portion, showing number
41   Baionnette Mle 89, standard pattern, by August Francotte & Cie of Liège
42   Obverse guard and ricasso of 41
43   Scabbard Mle 89, army pattern
44   Baionnette Mle 89, Garde Civique Cycliste, number U7273; 15.5mm muzzle ring
45   Scabbard Mle 89, Garde Civique
46   Baionnette Mle 24, number 5935 G Ie, probably made by Fabrique Nationale
47   Obverse guard and ricasso of 46
48   Épée-Baionnette Mle 16, Gendarmerie type, using Mle 82 blade

Canada

09. Ross bayonets, 1907–1916

Canada was the only member of the British Empire to design and adopt her own military rifle in preference to the Lee-Enfield; the history of the Ross Rifles has been covered in the four excellent articles that appeared in *Guns Review* in 1966 and by the book *Sir Charles Ross and his rifle* by Roger Phillips and Jerome Knap.

The first Ross rifle was produced as a sealed pattern in August 1902, but deliveries—although production began in 1903—were not made to the army until 1905. The Rifles, Ross, Mks 1 and 2 both had bayonet lugs (which may have been retrogressive modifications) but production of the bayonets did not begin until early 1909; hence the first rifles were not issued with bayonets.

Following correspondence between Ross and the Minister of Militia and Defence, a design was finally approved and patented in Canada in 1907. Consequently all Ross bayonets bear the inscription *Ross Rifle Co./Quebec/Patented 1907* on their pommels, and the patent was then granted in Britain in 1908.

The first Ross bayonet was designated the **Pattern 1908**, a term later changed to the **Bayonet, Ross Mk 1**. It has a heavy single-edged blade without fullers, approximately 260mm(10.25in) long though in some cases the dimensions vary. The back of the blade is rounded and the cutting edge is hollow-ground, while it ends in a blunt prow point reground in World War 1 to a more tapered pattern. The steel hilt has plain wood grips retained by two bolts, and the steel guard has a stepped-back muzzle ring some 14mm(0.551in) in diameter. A split annular spring is placed inside the muzzle ring with three contact points that allow a snug fit around the barrel and prevent rattling. Another spring is recessed within the pommel's bar attachment groove, the holding pin of which is clearly visible on the sides of the pommel. The pommels were stamped with the Canadian acceptance mark of a broad arrow within the letter 'C' and the date of manufacture, showing both month and year (*eg* '6-10' for June 1910).

Towards the end of World War 1, 20000 Mk 1 bayonets were sold to the USA as training weapons. These all have the mark *US* below the Board of Ordnance and Fortification's 'flaming bomb' on the grips and on the scabbard.

Production of the Mk 1 bayonet lasted only until 1910, for in 1911 the bayonet was altered to fit the Rifle Ross Mk 2** and reappeared under the title **Bayonet, Ross Mk 2**. The springs in the guard had been discarded—they had in any case been little more than an apology for the excessive manufacturing tolerances under which the rifles had initially been made—and the muzzle ring was enlarged to 16.5mm(0.650in) without the step-back. The Mk 2 bayonet was slightly modified in 1912 by riveting the guard to the tang instead of brazing it, and the design then remained unchanged until October 1915 when the final version was put into production. This, still designated Mk 2, differed from the earlier patterns in that the pommel spring was eliminated and the edges of the groove were bevelled. These bayonets were manufactured from the start with the pointed blade and remained bright-finished until March 1916, when they were phosphate coated.

Ross bayonets were also manufactured for British use, all of which have phosphated blades. The Mk 2 examples used by Britain bear neither a date nor the Canadian acceptance mark, and have instead a small War Department broad arrow over a typical Enfield inspector's mark (crown/E/number). Some Ross rifles and bayonets were reissued in World War 2 to the RAF.

All scabbards were made of leather with the tip of the internal chape showing. A leather belt frog was attached to the steel mouthpiece by a single staple placed at the back and there are two types, Mks 1 and 2, which differ in the size of the belt loop. The external dimensions are similar, but the stitching on the Mk 1 scabbard is taken much farther up the frog and thus forms a much narrower gap for the belt. The Ross Rifle Company did not make the scabbards and instead bought them from Hugh Carson Company Limited of Ottawa, who also manufactured replacements during World War 2.

49-55

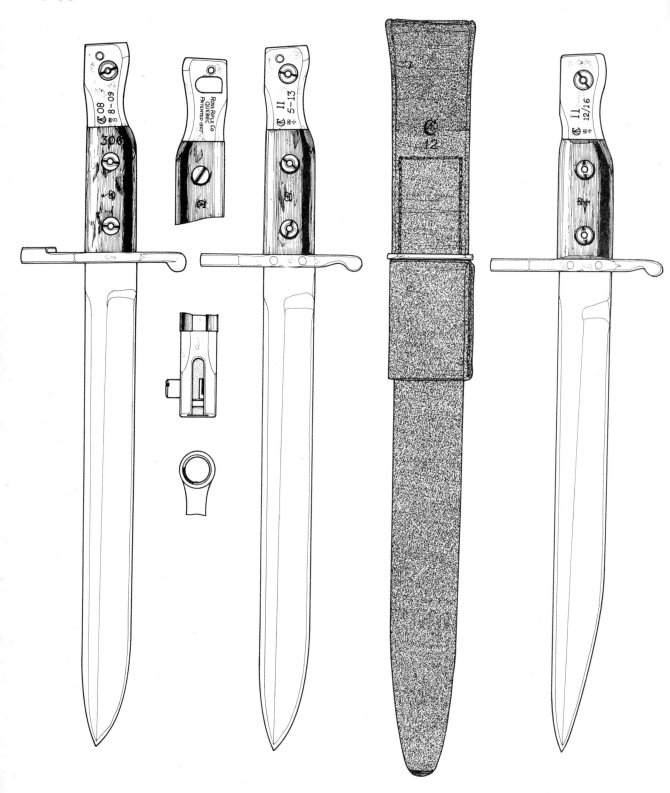

Czechoslovakia

10. Knife and sword bayonets, 1923

Czechoslovakia emerged from World War 1 as a new state, and the possessor of the old Austro-Hungarian weapons centres of Brno and Plzen (*i.e.* Pilsen, home of Skoda-Werke); the Czechs quickly established a modern small arms industry which grew to occupy a position of world fame in the 1920s and the 1930s. The most famous firm to emerge was Československá Zbrojovka aciová spoleĉnost Brno (Ĉs zbrojovka a s Brno, or simply ZB), who emerged in 1924 from the Československá statní zbrojovka, or 'Czech state factory', of 1919. At the beginning of the 1920s, the Czechs obtained machinery from the Germans to manufacture Mauser rifles, a form of war reparation, and after the appearance of several semi-experimental weapons the puská vz/98/22 (rifle model 98/22) was marketed. The bayonet adopted for the rifle was called by the Czechs the **bodák vz/23 dlouhý, výrobni vz/98/22 dlouhý**—the model 23 bayonet, manufacturing pattern 98/22—which gives an insight to the double terminology used by the manufacturers: one a designation of the introduction date (1923), and the other a 'manufacturing pattern' noting the rifle for which the bayonets were intended. The bayonet has a blade of 400mm(15.75in) with a typical reversed-edge blade sharpened along the top rather than along the bottom, and a typical Czech hilt with wood grips attached by two domed-head bolts. The crossguard has a muzzle ring of 15mm(0.591in) diameter and is riveted to the tang; the pommel has a typical Mauser bar-attachment slot and an internal coil-spring press-stud assembly. The overall length was originally 534mm(21.02in): bayonets made before the introduction of the vz/24 have a hilt length of 134mm(5.28in)—some 2mm longer than that of the later weapon—but this manufacturing distinction was lost on vz/23 long bayonets made after c.1926 when the hilt was made the same length as that of the vz/24. Thus the overall length of the post-1926 vz/23 is 532mm(20.94in).

A short bayonet, officially known as the **bodák vz/23 krátký, výrobni vz/98/22 krátký**, was also introduced in 1923: the blade of this was a mere 250mm(9.84in) long, which gave the short design an overall length of 384mm(15.19in) prior to 1926 and 382mm(15.04in) afterwards.

In 1929 a further change was made to the design of the 1923 long bayonet, achieved simply by reversing the blade so that it has a conventional 'underside edge': the result was the **bodák vz/23 dlouhý, výrobni vz/98/29 dlouhý**, the dimensions and design of which were those of the earlier vz/23 long bayonet second pattern (with the short hilt).

All three bayonets have blued steel scabbards and have the blades marked with the initials *ČSZ*, for Československá statní zbrojvký or 'Czech state manufacture', together with the lion of Bohemia which was used as the Czech crest.

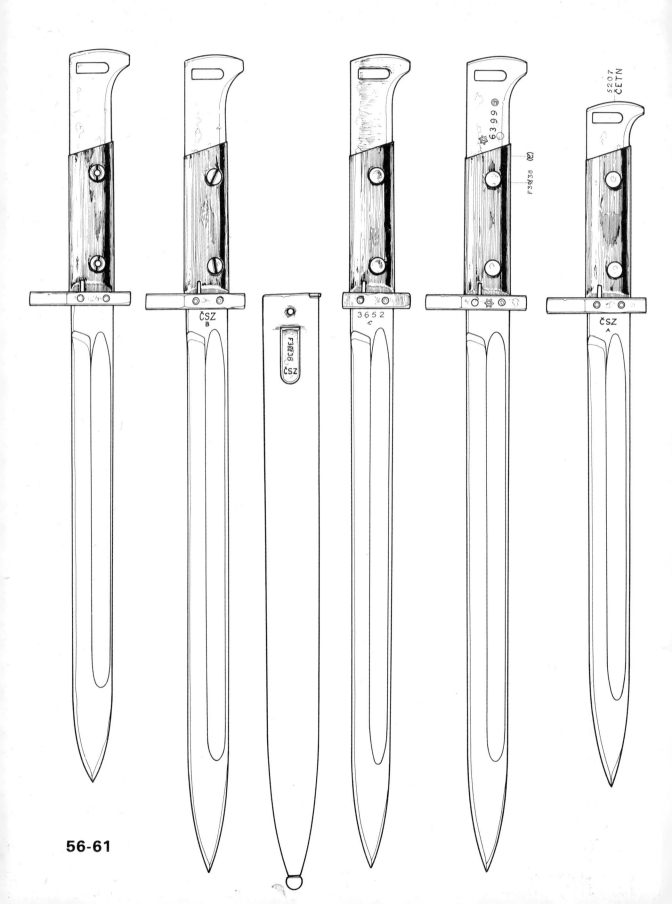

56-61

11.   Knife bayonet, 1924

The principal Czech service bayonet was the **bodák vz/24**, introduced c.1925/6 to accompany the vz/24 short rifle which was ultimately distributed in many countries throughout the world. The design of the vz/24 was essentially similar to that of the vz/23 bayonets that had preceded it, with a reversed-edge blade in old Austro-Hungarian style, a typically-Czech steel hilt with wood grips secured by domed-head rivets, a Mauser bar-attachment groove, a conventional internal coil-spring press-stud, and a muzzle ring of 15.5mm(0.610in) diameter. Those bayonets actually used by Czechoslovakia have the letter *ČSZ* stamped on the blade, and elsewhere on the frog-stud and on the back of the bayonet hilt, together with the lion of Bohemia and the date of manufacture. Most blades and scabbards are blued, although the hilts of a few were bright-finished.

During the German occupation of Czechoslovakia, many bayonets and rifles were seized and issued to the Wehrmacht: the bayonets thus taken were altered by the removal of the muzzle ring in keeping with standard German practice, as this part was found to be unnecessary provided that the long Mauser-style attachment bar was present on the rifle. New bayonets were then produced without the ring. These weapons usually have the German Waffenamt inspection marks stamped on the pommel (in the form of a stylised displayed eagle accompanied by the legend *WaA 836*, one of the Brno inspection offices) and on the frog-stud, together with the three-letter

SUPPLIES OF ZB-MADE RIFLES ABROAD, PRE-1940

date: country:nature of supplies

1925-30: Yugoslavia: vz/24 rifles and bayonets
1926: Lithuania: vz/24/26 special carbine, with vz/23 short bayonets (?)
1926: Turkey: vz/98 rifles (refurbished German Gew 98 type) with ex-German bayonets and vz/98/22 rifles with vz/23 long bayonets
1929: Mexico: vz/12 short rifles with Mexican sword bayonets (M95) not made in Czechoslovakia
1929-30: Siam (Thailand): vz/24 rifles and bayonets
1930: Peru: vz/24 rifles and bayonets
1930: Colombia: vz/12 short rifles, with Colombian FN Mle 24-type bayonets, not made in Czechoslovakia
1930: Venezuela: vz/24 rifles and bayonets
1930: Bolivia: vz/24 rifles and bayonets
1930-31: China: vz/98/22 rifles and vz/23 long bayonets
1930-31: Iran (Persia): vz/98/29 rifles and carbines with vz/23 long bayonets
1931: Brazil: vz/24 rifles and bayonets
1931: Estonia: vz/24 special carbines with vz/95 (*i.e.* old Austro-Hungarian) knife bayonets
1934: Brazil: vz/08/33 rifles and vz/12/33 carbines, with vz/23 long bayonets
1934: Peru: vz/32 short rifles and vz/24 bayonets
c. 1935: Colombia: vz/24 rifles and bayonets
c.1935: Ecuador: vz/24 rifles and bayonets
c.1935: Salvador: vz/24 rifles and bayonets
c.1935: Guatemala: vz/24 rifles and bayonets
c.1935: Nicaragua: vz/24 rifles and bayonets
1935: Latvia: vz/24 rifles and bayonets
1937: Uruguay: vz/32 short rifles and vz/23 short bayonets(?)
c.1937: Romania: vz/24 rifles and bayonets
1938: China: vz/24 rifles and bayonets
1938: Iran: vz/98/29 rifles and carbines with vz/23 long bayonets, and vz/24 rifles and bayonets

manufacturers' codes *dot, dou* and *dov*—representing the various branches of the Brno works, known by the Germans as Waffenwerke Brünn AG. Some bayonets have standard German-style securing bolts with slotted heads. A few scabbards were also modified by reversing the mouthpiece so that the bayonets fit into the scabbard facing to the left. The 'muzzle ring' vz/24 bayonets are more common than those without.

Many countries bought the Czech vz/24 rifles (see table), but only Yugoslavia manufactured her own vz/24 rifles (known in Yugoslavia as the pattern of 1929) together with FN Mle 24-type bayonets, all of which were made in the state arsenal at Kragujevač. The original Czech bayonets supplied to Yugoslavia are usually recognisable by the flush-grinding of the guard rivets and by the addition to the guard of a large four-figure serial number (sometimes preceded by a cyrillic letter).

Many Czech vz/24 bayonets were supplied to Israel, especially in the period immediately after the foundation of the Israeli state in 1947. Most of these are stamped with a star of David (six-point) on the crossguard and the frog-stud, together with the Israeli Defence Force inspectors' stamp and the army property stamp; many will also be found with a long Hebrew inscription above the stud, applied by the Haganah terrorist organisation when it was fighting the British and others during the British mandate in Palestine.

12. Knife bayonet, 1933

The Czechs also used a second pattern of knife bayonet, officially known as the **bodák vz/33 pro četnictvo a financní stráz, výrobni vz/16/33** (*i.e.* bayonet for gendarmes and financial guards model 33, manufacturing pattern 16/33). This differed from the vz/24 in the length of the pommel, and hence of the bar-attachment groove, which was some 23mm(0.91in) less; this gave the bayonet an overall length of 361mm(14.21in), but its design was otherwise that of the earlier 1923 (98/22) and 1924 weapons, with a reversed-edge blade and a wood-gripped steel hilt.

The vz/33 bayonet, which was issued with a carbine called the krátká cetnicá puska vz/33 ('short gendarmes' rifle model 33'), is very scarce. It seems that the total manufacture of the gun was in the region of 25 311: 18 040 were acquired in 1933/4, 5300 of which went to the financial guards and the rest to the gendarmerie, while a further 72/1 (split 2271:5000) were acquired in 1938. It is thus unlikely that more than 30 000 of the bayonets were manufactured. The Germans are known to have removed the muzzle rings from a few, probably more by way of an experiment, but the shortened bar-attachment groove—compared to that of the vz/24—would scarcely have been adequate. The bayonets were issued in blued all-steel scabbards.

62   Bodák vz/58, number D5061, with wood grips
63   Bodák vz/58, number a4664, with plastic-impregnated wood fibre grips
64   Scabbard, vz/58

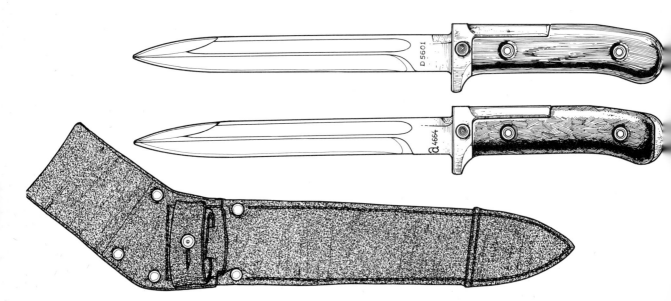

13. Knife bayonet, 1958

The late 1940s and the early 1950s saw the Czechs striving to design an ideal self-loading/automatic rifle with which to arm their own troops and with which to attract contracts from abroad. Various patterns were produced, mostly the designs of the Koucký brothers (whose weapons' designations were preceded by the letters ZK), the state firearms factory (ČZ), or Kyncla (ZJ). These were equipped with a motley collection of strange bayonets: the ZK 420, in at least one of its versions, was fitted with an under-barrel folding bayonet swinging in a vertical plane, the ČZ 502—the prototype of the vz/52—utilised a rod bayonet under the barrel, and the officially adopted *samočinna puska vz/52* used a peculiar laterally -swinging folding bayonet.

The vz/52 rifle, together with its unusual bayonet, was not a success and so the Czechs devised an assault rifle introduced under the designation *Samopal vz/58.* This, designed by Cermák, bears some external affinity with the Russian AK although internally there is no resemblance whatsoever. The Czechs also developed their own bayonet, the **bodák pro samopal vz/58**, which is strictly functional in conception.

Superficially it is a crude weapon, with a blade and hilt cast as a single piece using the lost-wax process—leaving the metal parts dull and of a rough finish. The short single-edged blade has a fuller on each side and a double-edged point, and there is a vestigial crossguard that does little to protect the hand when the weapon is used as a fighting knife. The press-stud is to be found on the reverse or left side of the guard. There is no muzzle ring and the bayonet is attached to the rifle by a unique but simple device, apparently first used on the ZK 472 of 1949, in

which the back of the hilt is for a large part taken up by a long attachment groove. The opening faces towards the blade, the opposite of conventional practice, and the barrel of the vz/58 assault rifle has a foresight cover below which is a long attachment bar. The bayonet is engaged by pushing it forwards onto the bar from the back, whereafter the catch springs in front of the attachment bar to hold the bayonet securely to the gun. The grips form the bulk of the hilt and completely encircle the tang for all but the bar groove on the back of the hilt.

Early examples of the vz/58 bayonet had wood grips at a time when the rifle also had a wooden stock. These are held in place by two steel rivets. More recent examples of the bayonet have grips of wood fibres impregnated with a translucent reddish-brown plastic, and the securing rivets are countersunk and covered by discs of the same material: the rivets are hence all but invisible, and a final coating of clear varnish ensures that the whole unit is waterproof. The overall length of the bayonet is 278mm(10.94in) of which 168mm(6.61in) represents the blade, and the scabbard is made entirely of stitched and riveted leather. There is a loop and a press-fastener to ensure that the hilt of the bayonet is securely held, and the integral belt frog is attached at an angle to position it perfectly for quick withdrawal. Later examples have the frog reinforced with stitching between the rivets.

The vz/58 bayonet combines a crude finish with a simple (if unusual) design: in theory the attachment system is very poor, because the stress caused in the bayonet by a thrust is taken entirely on the catch—in most weapons it is taken by the solid steel of the guard end of the attachment groove and thus releases the catch from undue strain—but it is probable that in practice the Czechs are happy to accept ease of production in preference to theoretical strength: the times on which the bayonet is actually used as such are likely to be rare.

Denmark

14. Knife bayonet, 1889

The Danes were the first to adopt the Krag-Jørgensen

rifle, designed by two Norwegians, which was issued in 1889 as the Gevaer m/1889; small modifications were made in 1908 (the addition of Barry's safety catch) and in 1910 (improved ammunition and a re-graduated rearsight) but the rifles remained in service until World War 2.

The short knife bayonet, known as the *Knivbajonet m/1889,* was attached to a lug on the barrel jacket and did not have a muzzle ring owing to the fact that the length of the slot sufficed to give rigidity to the mounting. The blade is 228mm (9.00in) long and ends in a double-edged point; there are shallow fullers some 150mm (5.88in) long on each side of the blade. The entire unit—blade, rudimentary crossguard and hilt—are manufactured as a single forging which ensured that the m/1889, although weighing no more than 227gm (8.00oz), was strong enough to withstand the rigours of active service. A spring-loaded catch, actuated by means of a pivoted press-stud protruding from the pommel, retained the rifle's T-lug in the attachment groove. The m/1889 grips were originally of chequered leather, but this was found to rot in wet conditions and those bayonets made after 1892 were wood-gripped.

The steel-mounted leather scabbard has a loop for the belt frog and a catch on the side of the topmount, used to hold the bayonet firmly in the scabbard by locking over the crossguard. This device was later copies by both the Americans and the Norwegians.

Many m/1889 rifles were shortened to provide carbines, consequent to the 'short rifle craze' begun by the British SMLE and the American Springfield: the Danish weapons were issued with the m/1915 sword bayonet, which meant that quantities of the short m/1889 were declared surplus. Some of these were converted in 1923 to provide the **Kniv for befalingsmaend m/1923,** a knife for officers and NCOs. In these the locking mechanism was removed and the attachment slot filled with iron; many also had a shortened hilt.

Most m/1889 bayonets were made in Denmark by either Haerens Tøjhus (1915-23) or Haerens

Rustkammer (1923-32), and are so marked on the blades. Some were also made prior to World War 1 by Weyersberg, Kirschbaum & Cie of Solingen (whose trademark, a king's head and a knight's helm, appeared on the blade). The pommels often bear regimental marks and the crossguards are stamped with the date of manufacture — a crown over 11, for example, signifies 1911.

15. Sword bayonet, 1915

During World War 1 the Danes adopted a neutral status, but the proximity of Germany caused the Danish ordnance to reconsider their weapons with regard to those of the contemporary German army. Thus it was realised that the reach of the Gew 98/S98 combination was greater than that of the Gevaer m/1889-10 when fitted with the Knivbajonet m/1889, and so the Danes designed a light sword bayonet known as the **Kårdebajonet m/1915.** At the close of the war however, after quantities of the m/1915 had been produced, the whole question of bayonets' usefulness was reconsidered and the sword bayonet was thereafter issued with the various 1889-system carbines: the m/1889 bayonet was reissued with the full-length rifles. The issue of the bayonets was as follows:

Gevaer m/1889 (including m/1889-08 and m/1889-10). Knivbajonet m/1889 until 1915, Kårdebajonet m/1915 in the period 1915-22, Knivbajonet m/1889 thereafter.

Rytterkarabin m/1889 (cavalry carbine). This was adopted in 1912, but was not fitted with a bayonet bar until 1923, when the Kårdebajonet m/1915 was added.

Ingeniørkarabin m/1889 (engineers' carbine). This,

65   Bayonet m/1889 by Weyersberg, Kirschbaum & Cie of Solingen, 1890; with marks of the 13th battalion
66   Scabbard m/1889
67   Bayonet m/1889, by RKV of Købnhavn (Copenhagen), 1911; number 83102, with marks of the 29th battalion—
       cancelled—and the 40th battalion
68   Bayonet m/1915, by Haerens Tøjhus, 1917; number 111291, mark of 13th battalion
69   Scabbard m/1915

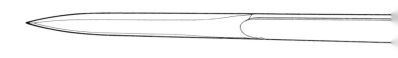

introduced in 1918, was fitted to take the m/1915 bayonet in 1923.

Fodfolkskarabin m/1889-24 (infantry carbine). This was fitted to take the m/1915 bayonet on its introduction in 1924.

Artillerikarabin m/1889-24 (artillery carbine). This, too, was fitted to take the m/1915 on its introduction.

The Kårdebajonet (sword bayonet) has a slim tapering T-backed blade, 455mm (17.78in) long, finished bright and similar in shape to the French Mle 74 (Gras). It has a single cutting edge and a strong narrow point ideal for thrusting. The slender hilt has plain wood grips inset in the steel and secured by two brass rivets. The diameter of the muzzle ring is 14mm (0.551in) but there is no real crossguard, with the exception of a protrusion that serves to retain the bayonet in the scabbard by engaging the scabbard catch. There is a conventional bar attachment groove, stretching the length of the hilt, and an internal coil-spring press-stud assembly (about one third of the way along the hilt from the pommel.

The slim leather scabbard has steel mounts, the top of which has a steel loop for the frog and a spring-loaded catch to retain the bayonet.

The weapons are very clearly marked, which facilitates exact indentification. Below the muzzle ring is stamped the name or initials of the manufacturer; a crowned *HV* shows that the weapon was the product of Haerens Vaabenarsenal (1932-43), while the earlier marks *Haerens Tøjhus* (1915-23) and *Haerens Rustkammer* (1923-32) are usually stamped in full. The bayonet's fabrication number is on the reverse of the crossguard, while the date of manufacture is often to be found on the pommel. Thus a crowned 17 shows that the bayonet was made in 1917. Furthermore, the army markings can also often be found on the pommel: the Danish army was divided into battalions, so that *13 B 621* would have been the 621st weapon of the 13th Battalion.

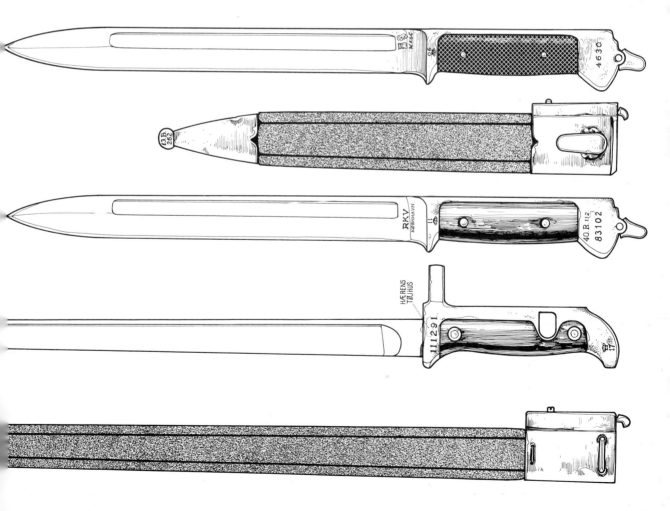

France

16.   Sabre bayonets, 1840–1859

During the mid-nineteenth century France recovered her position as Europe's leading military nation, and until her defeat in 1871 by Prussia many nations—including Britain and the United States—emulated the French army. Uniforms, sidearms and bayonets were copied, and French-style yataghan-blade sabre bayonets were quickly adopted throughout the world.

The original French model was the **Sabre Baionnette Mle 1840**, which had a yataghan blade of 510mm(20.08in) and a cast-brass hilt with fifteen ribs. The brass crossguard, of recurved type, was soon found to be easily damaged and so the weapon had a very short service life.

The **Sabre Baionnette Mle 1842** was similar to its predecessor except that the weak brass guard was replaced by one of wrought iron, while the blade was lengthened to 570mm(22.44in). The Mle 42 bayonet was attached to the rifle by means of a bar on the muzzle which mated with the T-slot cut into the back of the bayonet's hilt; the first part of the bar slotted into the T-groove while the long bar extension fitted into the shallow groove running the length of the hilt-back. This effectively steadied the bayonet on the barrel and prevented undue strain on the muzzle ring.

In 1859 the Mle 42 was modified by the supersession of the catch and external leaf-spring assembly in favour of an internally-sprung unit, whose rectangular press-stud protruded from the reverse or left side of the pommel. At the same time the position of the scabbard blade-retaining springs was changed from one of gripping the flats of the blade to one of gripping the edges—which did nothing to maintain the condition of the edge. The revised bayonet, often known as the Mle 42/59, was officially known as the **Sabre Baionnette Mle 42 transformée**.

All three types of sabre bayonet were issued in all-steel scabbards of standard French pattern, each bearing frog loops rather than frog-studs. The bayonets were worn in the period 1840-66 by NCOs and élite troops, as badges of rank and privilege, and could be taken away as a punishment.

The Mle 40 bayonet was issued with the Carabine Mle 40, while the Mle 42 and Mle 42 T fitted a variety of guns, amongst them the Carabines Mle 42, Mle 46 and Mle 53 and the Mousqueton Mle 29 T. The majority of French troops were equipped with triangular-blade socket bayonets, while NCOs and élite units had previously also worn the clumsy shortswords discarded with the advent of the sabre bayonets.

French weapons of this era are easy to date from the scriptic markings along the blade backs; a specimen can, for example, be marked *Mre. Impale. de Châtt . Obre. 1861 S.B. Mle 1842*, an abbreviation of 'Manufacture Imperiale de Châtellerault, Octobre 1861, Sabre Baionnette Modèle 1842' showing that the weapon was made in October 1861 in the royal manufactory at Châtellerault. Despite the fact that the designation says 'Mle 1842', the weapon is a Mle 42 T.

17.   Sabre-lance and épée bayonets, 1854–1858

When Louis Napoleon was proclaimed emperor in 1852, he reorganised the army and restored much of its past magnificence. In March 1854 L'Escadron Des Cent Gardes was formed to act as the emperor's bodyguard, equipped as cuirassiers, and in May the Garde Impériale was reinstated. The dragoons of the Garde Impériale were equipped with a triple-purpose bayonet that served the purpose of sabre, lance and bayonet. A similar weapon was issued to the Cent Gardes and the weapons were carried on horseback in the manner of cavalry sabres. A shorter épée bayonet was also issued to the Cent Gardes, but no documentation has been found to say for certain why and by whom it was carried.

The original Cent Gardes bayonet rejoices under the unlikely title **Sabre Lance du Mousqueton des Cent Gardes Treuille de Beaulieu, Modèle 1854**; the double-fullered blade was provided, in concept at least, by some earlier French heavy cavalry sabres and has double fullers on each side. The pommel and the guard are of brass, the former possessing a T-groove, and lock is effected by an internally-sprung press stud. The handguard is wide and flat, slightly swept back at the quillon, while the muzzle ring is squared at the top to fit over the firearm's foresight. The grooved one-piece grip is made of horn and has a steel tang along the back, which is attached to the pommel by a round retaining screw; removal of the screw permits the hilt to be dismantled. The blade is no less than 1000mm(39.37in) long and the steel scabbard is of steel with two suspension rings. The scabbard is, in fact, very similar to that of the Mle 1816 heavy cavalry sabre.

A lighter épée bayonet is known to have been issued to the Cent Gardes, although it is by no means clear when such issue occurred. Basically the weapon, known simply as the **Épée Baionnette Des Cent Gardes**, is a much-lightened version of the Mle 54: owing to the carbine-like 'rifle' with which the Cent Gardes were armed, it is likely that the original Mle 54 was too heavy for the gun. The effect of the massive bayonet on such a fragile gun cannot have been anything but disastrous, and it may thus be that the light épée bayonet dates from c.1858-60. The hilt is of brass and black horn, in the style of that of the Mle 54, but the whole is much lighter in construction. The smaller and lighter blade, 600mm(23.62in) long with a maximum width at the hilt of 26mm(1.02in), is deeply fullered on the sides and grooved on the back. The scabbard for this weapon is assumed to be of steel, but none has yet been found.

The special bayonet of the imperial guard was called the **Sabre Lance du Fusil de Dragon de la Garde Impériale, Modèle 1858**, and was patterned on the Mle 1816 heavy cavalry sabre. The hilt has a grip of horn and a four-bar brass guard, which has the muzzle ring in its upper part. The pommel incorporates a similar press-stud and spring assembly to that of the Mle 54 Cent Gardes bayonet. The blade, again of 1000mm(39.37in), has two deep fullers on each side while the steel scabbard has two suspension rings.

The two Sabre Lance bayonets were extraordinarily clumsy when fitted to the rifle, but they made quite passable sabres—just as the British cutlass bayonets were effective when used as hand weapons. The three are the rarest of the French bayonets, of interesting appearance and of considerable significance in the history of weapons of this class.

18.   Sabre bayonet, 1866

The French sabre bayonet of 1866, officially known as the **Sabre Baionnette Modèle 1866 Série 'Z'**, was the accessory of the Chassepot needle-gun—the principal French firearm of the Franco-Prussian war. The weapon is basically a much-lightened derivative of the Mle 42 and Mle 42 T sabre bayonets, with a slimmer yataghan blade, a newly-designed cast-brass hilt and a leaf-spring press-stud unit. The steel guard has a long swept forward quillon that ends in a disc finial, while the guard's muzzle ring incorporates an adjustable screw and a small cut-out that accommodates a small tenon on the rifle's muzzle (which is diametrically opposed to the bayonet bar). The Mle 66's blade is about 580mm(22.83in) long and the steel scabbard has a frog loop in standard French style.

The original French bayonets can be recognised by their blade-back markings, which fall into two distinct categories; those made in the period of the Deuxième Empire, or second empire, are prefaced by the abbreviations *Mre. Impale. de* while those made after the fall of Napoleon III—when France again became a republic—bear the marks *Mre. d'Armes de*. Each is followed by the place of manufacture, generally Châtellerault, St Etienne, Tulle or Mutzig, although several private firms are known to have been involved in the manufacture of Mle 66 bayonets prior to 1870.

After the fall of France to the Prussians and their allies, many weapons were handed to the victors as war indemnity: some Chassepot rifles were converted by the Germans to fire metallic-case ammunition, and quantities of Mle 66 bayonets were altered to fit the Gew 71 and placed in store alongside stocks of unconverted weapons. These, known by the Germans as the 'Französisches Chassepot-Gewehr Säbelbajonett', saw use prior to and in World War 1 in the hands of the Landwehr. Most have German marks in addition to the French originals. In most cases the French belt loop has been replaced on the scabbard by a German frog-stud.

The Mle 66 continued to be made for the French armies after the 1870/1 war and many were reissued for service in World War 1 with lines of

70   Sabre-baionnette Mle 42, made at Châtellerault in 1853
71   Scabbard, Mle 42 and Mle 42T
72   Sabre-baionnette Mle 42T (or Mle 42/59), made at Tulle
73   Épée-baionnette des Cent Gardes, lightened model, c.1858
74   Sabre-Lance du Fusil de Dragon de la Garde Impériale, Mle 58

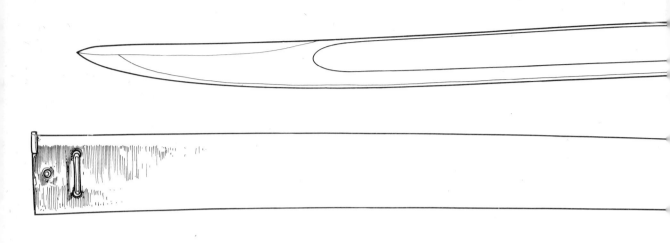

70-74

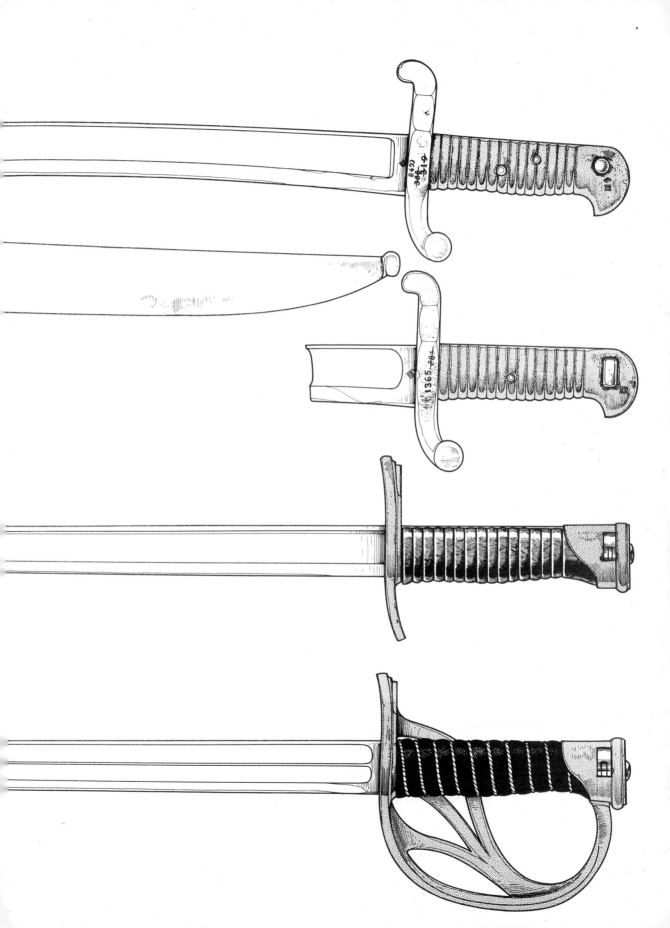

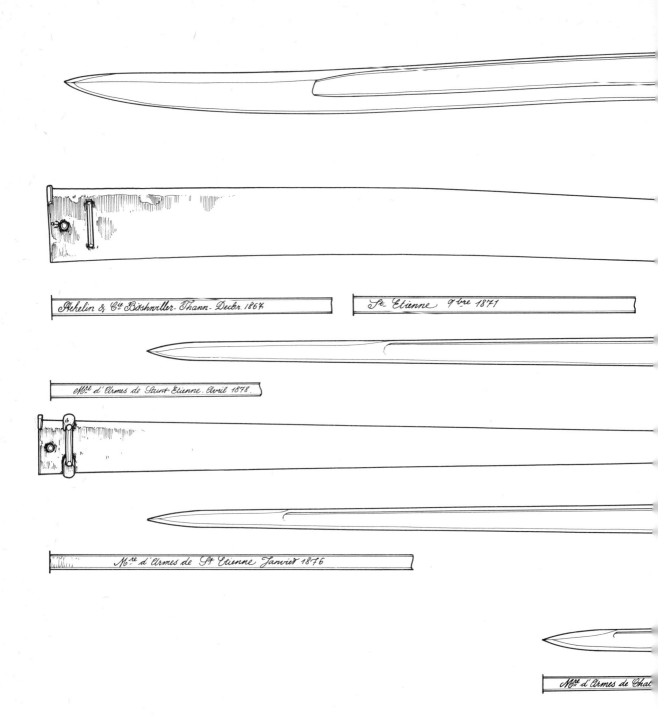

Achelin & Cⁱᵉ Bitshwiller-Thann- Decbr 1867.

Sᵗᵉ Etienne   9ᵇʳᵉ 1871

Mᵈˡ d'Armes de Saint-Etienne. Avril 1878.

Mᵈʳᵉ d'Armes de Sᵗ Etienne Janvier 1876

Mᵈʳᵉ d'Armes de Chat

75-89

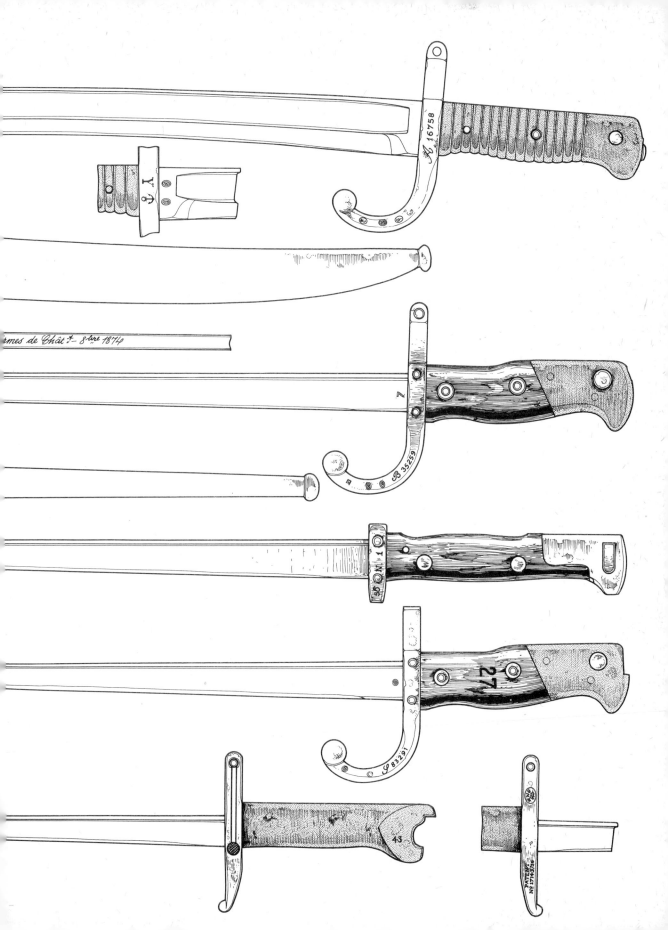

rmes de Chât.º – 8bre 1874

communication troops. Some even saw service in World War 2 in the hands of the Garde Nationale. An approximately three-quarter size version of the Mle 66, not always correct in detail, was issued to the Enfants de Troupe (cadets).

The Mle 66 influenced the weapons of many European powers, and there are other bayonets—the Dutch Beaumont, the Belgian Mle 68, and even the Bavarian Werder of 1869—which are scarcely more than direct copies of the French original. Quantities of essentially-similar bayonets were also made in Germany for use on the Remington rolling block rifles that achieved distribution throughout South America: Mle 66-type bayonets are as a result known in which there are no fullers, or two on each side, or even three short fullers on each side. Most of these defy identification.

The bayonet for the Egyptian Remington rolling block rifle, model 1867, is virtually a Chassepot and differs only in the design of the fullers (being German made), in the lack of the secondary tenon cut-out on the muzzle ring, and in the simple flat sides of the hilt-back groove: on the Mle 66 this is chamfered. Paradoxically, the German-made Egyptian Remington bayonet was supplied to France in time for the war. The Egyptians defaulted before the contract was fulfilled, and the undelivered arms were instead acquired by France. The Remington bayonets are, of course, much rarer than the Mle 66. The Egyptian contract was then fulfilled after the Franco-Prussian war.

19. Epée bayonets, 1874–1878

The Mle 74 épée bayonet can be called the first modern bayonet issued to the French army, for it replaced the clumsy sword bayonets of the previous three decades. The Mle 74 was designed by a commission headed by Général Basile Gras, whose name is usually attached to both the rifle and the bayonet, and was used with both the Fusil d'Infanterie Mle 74—a newly-made metallic-ammunition rifle—and the various conversions of the Mle 66 rifles which used the new cartridges.

The bayonet has a strong T-section blade, some 520mm(20.47in) long, with a short double edge at the point and a hilt with a brass pommel. The wood grips are retained by two rivets, one of which also acts to secure the leaf spring to the right or obverse side of the hilt. The steel guard has a swept forward quillon and is riveted to the tang.

The bayonet is attached to the rifle by a T-lug on the gun's muzzle engaging with a slot cut in the back of the pommel, while the slender extension bar on the lug slides along the hilt and engages with a small cut-out at the base of the muzzle ring. As the wood grips are not as strong as the solid brass of earlier weapons, they are shaped flush with the tang.

The oval steel scabbard was originally heavily blued and ends in a ball ferrule; it is also fitted with a frog loop. The Mle 74 bayonets are stamped along the blade backs with the place and date of manufacture, in typical French fashion, while the guard generally bears a serial number in the form of a five-figure number following a script letter: various inspection marks—poinçons de contrôle—are also liberally scattered over the weapon. The lighter weight of the Mle 74 made it easier to fire the rifle with the bayonet fixed.

A small-scale Mle 74, made by Andreux of Paris, was issued to the Enfants de Troupe; this is only some 515mm(20.28in) long with a blade of 420mm(16.54in). In addition, a bayonet similar to the Mle 74 was adopted in 1878 for the Austrian-designed Kropatschek navy rifle; this bayonet, the **Épée Baionnette du Fusil de la Marine Mle 78**, was identical to the Mle 74 with the exception of the hilt, which was slightly longer and had a flat back. These bayonets, most of which seem to have been made in Solingen by Alexander Coppel

75   Sabre-Baionnette Mle 66, number A16578, made by Stehelin & Cie in 1867
76   Obverse guard showing naval anchor mark
77   Scabbard Mle 66
78   Blade mark: Stehelin & Cie, Bitschwiller/Thann, December 1867
79   Blade mark: St Etienne, October 1871
80   Blade mark: Manufacture d'Armes de Châtellerault, November 1874
81   Epée-Baionnette Mle 74, number B35259, made at St Etienne in April 1878
82   Blade mark of 81
83   Scabbard, Mle 74
84   Epée-Baionnette Mle 74, rehilted by the Germans c.1915/16; originally made at St Etienne
85   Blade mark of 84
86   Epée-Baionnette Mle 74, shortened and with the muzze ring bushed for unknown purposes
87   Blade mark of 86 —Manufacture d'Armes de Châtellerault, 1877
88   Pritchard-Greener revolver bayonet, using part of an Mle 74 blade, 1916
89   Obverse guard

& Cie, are often found marked with an anchor device.

The Greek government also adopted the Gras rifle (the bayonet was also used with the native designed 'Mylonas' rifle) but purchased their arms from Österreichische Waffenfabrik-Gesellschaft at Steyr. France had also bought some of her arms from Steyr, but the markings of the two differ: Greek Mle 74 bayonets bear the legend *Waffenfabrik Steyr* and a date, while the French issue are marked *Usine de Steyr* and a date.

Many Gras bayonets were captured and used by the Germans in World War 1, some of which had the entire hilt removed and replaced by an Ersatz pattern of brass or steel. This then fitted the Gew 98, but others were modified in Belgian factories to permit the Mle 74 bayonets to fit the Gew 71, the Gew 71/84 and the Gew 88: most of these had alterations made to the muzzle rings by grinding, and a few had the press-stud moved from the left or reverse side to the right or obverse. Many then had the blade bent out of the line of fire, owing to the angle at which the bayonets fitted the different muzzle of the German rifles.

Perhaps the most interesting modification to the Mle 74 was the World War 1 invention of Captain Arthur Pritchard who, with the co-operation of the W W Greener firm, designed a knife bayonet to fit the Webley Mk 6 service revolver. The brass, or occasionally steel, hilt made use of the last 210mm(8.27in) of the Mle 74 blade and was carried in the lower portion of a Gras scabbard. Few of these bayonets, whose utility was in any case questionable, were made: many of those now in existence were completed after the war from parts on hand.

20. Epée bayonets, 1886–1935

When the French adopted the Fusil d'Infanterie Modèle 1886—the famous Lebel—they also adopted one of the most famous bayonets issued and which, with modifications, continued in use throughout both world wars as the standard infantry bayonet. The original Mle 86 bayonet had a tapering cruciform blade of 520mm(10.47in) which fitted into a similarly-shaped tubular steel scabbard fitted with a belt-loop. The **Épée-Baionnette Modèle 86** had a white-metal hilt screwed onto the blade tang and secured by the same screw that governed the movement of the press-stud. The steel guard was made with a swept forward quillon and a 15mm(0.591in) muzzle ring. Bayonet press-studs are normally placed on the pommel, but the Mle 86 bayonets had the stud within the guard operating a catch behind the muzzle ring. A groove along the back of the hilt mated with a bar on the rifle's barrel and—finally—the round raised portion of the pommel fitted into a recess on the nosecap.

The first modification made to the Mle 86 simply improved the method of attaching the hilt to the blade tang. A separate round nut screwed onto the end of the tang and fitted flush with the pommel, making removal of the white-metal hilt considerably easier as the original design sometimes caused damage to the soft metal when the grip was forcibly unscrewed.

Another minor modification was made in 1893, at the same time as the modified Mle 86/93 rifle was adopted. The bayonet's press-stud was redesigned so that the chequered surface was flatter and slightly easier to manufacture. The result was known as the **Épée-Baionnette Mle 86/93**.

During World War 1 more improvements were made with the adoption of the **Épée-Baionnette Mle 86/93/16**. The press-stud was again redesigned and the bayonets were manufactured without the quillon. Some Mle 86 and Mle 86/93 bayonets were modified by removing the quillon, but the majority escaped this alteration. The two altered types, 'pre-1916' and 'post-1916', cannot be confused; the former has a curved side (facing the blade) from which the quillon was removed, while the latter has a rectangular form. Most of the bayonets made during and after 1916 had brass hilts in place of the earlier white-metal type. A small quantity was produced using the stocks of white-metal hilts held by the arsenals, and a few were made with blued steel hilts.

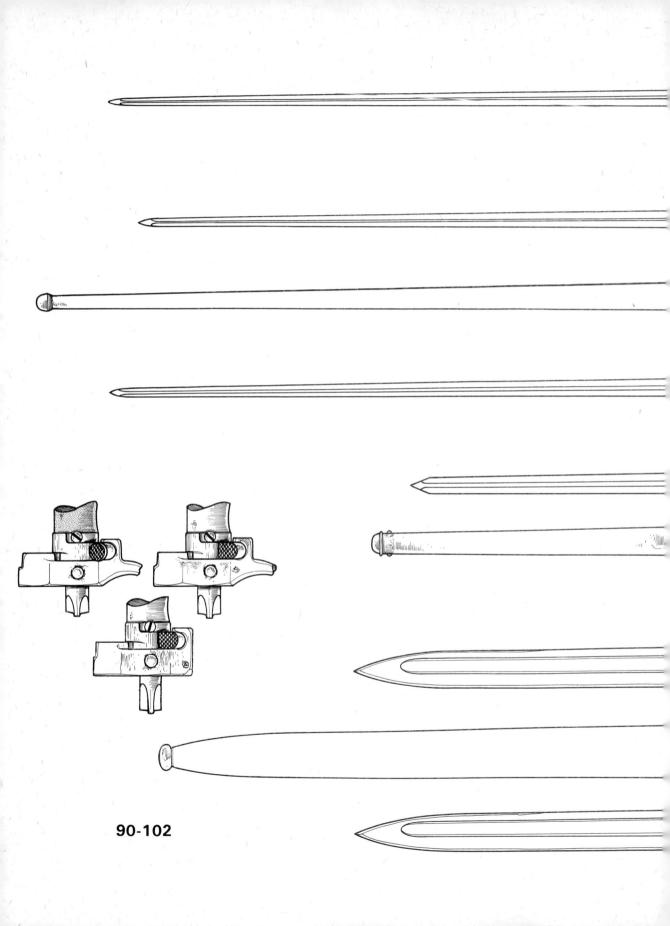

90-102

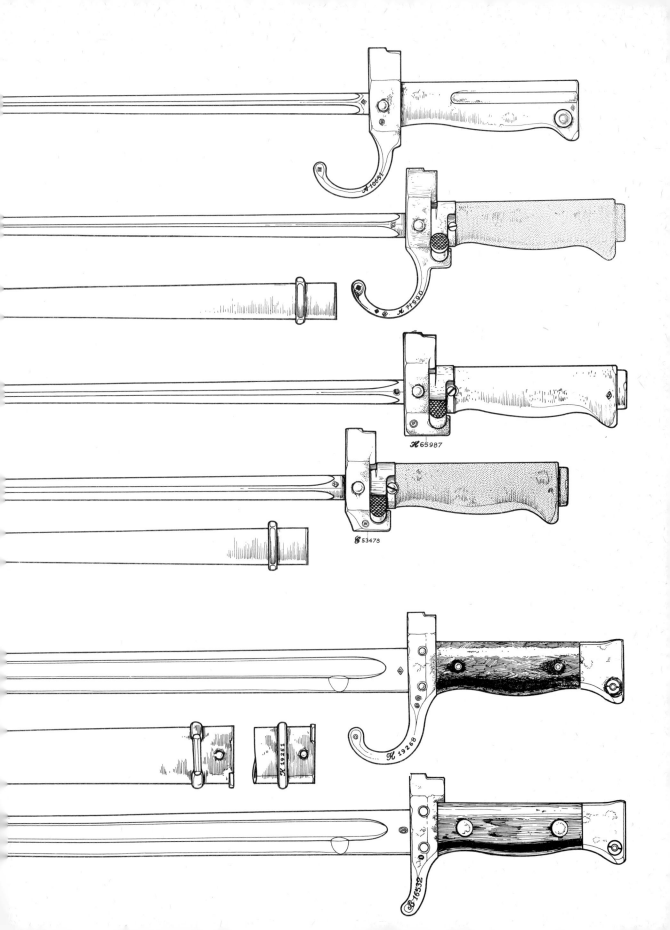

The final official modification did not appear until 1935, when many examples of all the variations had the blades shortened to 335mm(13.19in). The scabbards were similarly modified to fit the shorter blade. Many odd blade lengths can be found which are *not* official '/35' weapons; most are simply bayonets which broke during the war and which were repointed and reissued with blades of varying lengths, depending where the break occurred.

Thousands of Lebel bayonets were sold to Turkey after World War 1 but these remained unaltered from the original and bore no distinctive marks. Captured bayonets were issued to German reserves and these sometimes have a regimental marking stamped onto the hilt. Polish troops fighting during World War 1 with the Russians, and with the Free French during the last war, were equipped with Lebel rifles and bayonets; the latter may be found stamped *WZ 86* or *WZ/86/93*. Many other troops equipped by the French carried these arms, including Imperial Russian troops on the Macedonian front during World War 1.

A miniature Mle 86 bayonet was made and issued to Enfants de Troupe (Cadets), and though these vary considerably they are approximately 480mm(18.90in) long with a blade of about 385mm(15.16in). Often inaccurate in detail, they were simply small-scale versions of the infantry bayonet.

Another bayonet utilising the same 520mm(20.5in) cruciform blade was the **Épée-Baionnette de Gendarmerie Modèle 90**, which also had a white-metal hilt. It differs from the Mle 86 in that there is a concave groove along the reverse or left side of the hilt for three-quarters of its length. The press-stud was placed at the end of the pommel to operate a catch within a round hole. These bayonets were also shortened in 1935 and were issued with the Carabine de Gendarmerie Mle 90.

The metal surfaces of the Lebel bayonets were usually left bright-finished, with the exception of those Mle 86/93/16 weapons with steel hilts—which were blued overall. All scabbards were blued.

21. Sword bayonets, 1892–1914

At the beginning of the 1890s, having become quickly dissatisfied with the performance of their Mle 86 (Lebel) rifles whose design had been quickly overtaken by those of other nations, the French began experiments with the guns of André Berthier. The result was the introduction in 1891 of three carbines and a short rifle, on purely limited scales, and in 1892 came the *Mousqueton d'Artillerie*

Modèle 92 together with a Gendarmerie carbine bearing the same year designation.

The **Sabre-baionnette Mle 92** is a well-balanced weapon, 515mm(20.28in) long with a blade of 400mm(15.75in); the blade is single-edged with a fuller on each side, and the last 150mm(5.91in) of the back is grooved to facilitate withdrawal after a thrust. Two notches on the fullers, close to the guard, engage the scabbard's blade-retaining springs to hold the bayonet firmly in place. The hilt has plain composition grips held by two steel rivets, and a sweptforward quillon: the small muzzle ring, whose diameter was 15.5mm(0.610in), also possesses a small square notch—facing towards the rear—which slides around the carbine's foresight.

The first pattern of the Mle 92 has a muzzle ring with a length of 15mm(0.63in), the same width as the guard which is held to the tang by two dome-headed rivets. There is no groove along the back of the hilt, because the attachment stud on the carbine's nosecap passes into a hole in the flat end of the pommel where it is engaged by the press-stud mechanism. The scabbard is of steel with a small round ferrule and a loop attachment for the belt frog; its overall length is 415mm(16.39in).

Before the turn of the century, the French introduced the second pattern of the Mle 92, which differed from the first in an extension of the muzzle ring to the rear—over the grips—which gave it a length of 19mm(0.75in). This was intended to give better support to the weapon when fixed around the carbine's foresight.

During the course of World War 1 the French promulgated an order officially shortening the quillons of the Mle 92 bayonets: the result, sometimes known as the **Sabre-baionnette Mle 92/15**, was also given wooden grips held by two large rivets. The old composition grips had often split along the line of the rivets, and so it was desirable to introduce a substitute. New bayonets were to be manufactured in this fashion while bayonets coming in for repair were to be suitably altered, but it is evident that the French never completely implemented their order and that bayonets were produced after the war *with* the full quillons.

The bayonets rarely bear more than a selection of French inspection marks together with a serial number consisting of one or two script letters followed by a four-figure number; a few of the bayonets produced prior to c.1895 can, however, be found with the abbreviation *Mre. d'Armes de Chât. Mai 1893* (in this case 'made at the Châtellerault arms factory in May 1893') but these are rare. Many Mle 92 carbines and bayonets were captured in World War 1 by the Germans, and issued (in many cases with Mle 86/93 or Mle 07/15 rifles, neither of which used the

Mle 92 bayonet) to Eisenbahn und Pioniertruppen—railway protection troops and pioneers. The bayonets were issued to them principally as sidearms, so it mattered little what rifle was carried. The German bayonets are often found stamped *Deutsch, Deutschland,* or simply with a displayed eagle property mark. Mle 92 bayonets, together with other French weapons of the period, were also used by Poland in the period prior to c.1922/5: these bear pommel stamps *W.Z.92,* the Polish word *wzor* being equivalent to 'model'.

Some confusion has arisen concerning the guns that utilised the Mle 92 and the Mle 92/15 bayonets: the design was only an accessory to the Mousquetons d'Artillerie Mle 92 and Mle 92/27, and to the essentially similar Mousquetons Mle 16 and Mle 16/27. The various Berthier-system rifles—Mle 02, Mle 07, Mle 07/15, and Mle 16—all used the standard Mle 86 épée bayonet. The Mousqueton de Gendarmerie Mle 92, essentially the same as the artillery carbine, also used the bayonet in preference to the earlier Mle 90 pattern.

Germany

22.   Sword bayonet, 1871

In 1871 Prussia, aided by the other German states, defeated France: Bismarck then united the German states into a federation and the king of Prussia became the Kaiser (emperor). In the same year, anxious to replace the Dreyse needle-guns, the ordnance authorities tested the rifle designed by Peter-Paul Mauser and on 9th December 1871 the gun was accepted as the Infanterie-Gewehr Modell 71. Changes made at Mauser's insistence then delayed final acceptance until 22nd March 1872, whereupon issues of the infantry rifle, a Jägerbüchse (the weapon of the riflemen) and a carbine were officially sanctioned.

The bayonet issued with the infantry rifle drew its inspiration from patterns that had passed before, especially the Füsilier-Seitengewehr of 1860, and was a well-made and well-balanced design. The 470mm(18.50in) blade, deeply fullered on both sides, is bright-finished and the steel crossguard is recurved in typically German fashion. The cast-brass hilt has a large steel rivet close to the guard to hold the hilt to the blade's tang, and the press-stud is operated by an external L-shape leaf spring on the right or obverse side of the hilt. This side of the hilt, and not the

reverse or left side, bears decoration in the form of seventeen diagonal striations cut into the brass. The muzzle ring diameter of these weapons is about 17.4mm(0.685in) although the dimension is subject to some variation.

A sawbacked version of the Infanterie-Seitengewehr 71 was issued to the NCOs, who constituted some 6% of the regimental strength: this weapon is not pioneer's issue (they used the Pionierfaschinenmesser 71 instead) and was solely for the use of the infantry. The number of double sawteeth varies between 22 and 27, depending on the manufacturer.

The bayonets were issued in brass-mounted leather scabbards, although there is a possibility that the first issues in Württemberg were accompanied by steel-mounted scabbards. A long brass frog-stud was used on all except Bavarian scabbards, which used a frog loop in the French style. A few early scabbards were also made in which the mounts were internal; these were stitched so that only the tip of the chape and the frog-stud protruded. In addition some all-steel scabbards were manufactured for the bayonets during World War 1, when a few ex-S71 blades were also converted by the addition of new wood-gripped hilts (for the Gew and Kar 98) or by the addition of an all-metal Ersatz hilt. These modifications were carried out in very limited quantities.

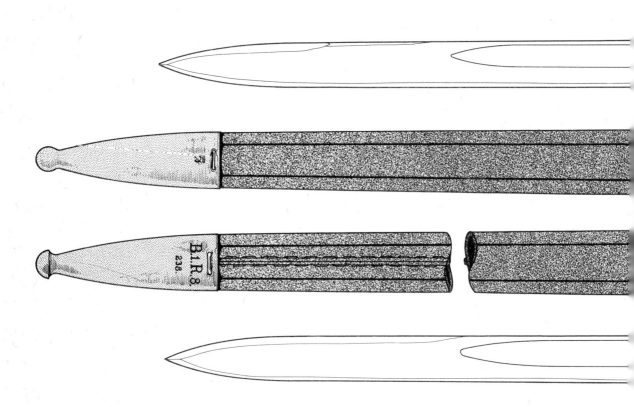

103 Seitengewehr Modell 1871 (S71), made by Ernst Wilhelm of Suhl in 1875; the guard bears the marks of 39. Reserve-
     Reiter Regiment
104 Scabbard, S71
105 Scabbard, S71, Bavarian pattern
106 Seitengewehr Modell 71, made by W.R. Kirschbaum & Cie of Solingen in 1879; the guard mark represents 24. Infanterie
     Regiment's fifth company
107 Pionierfaschinenmesser Modell 1871 (P71 or Pfm 71), Württemberg pattern: the guard mark is that of 13.Pionier-
     Bataillon 2. Festungs-Kompagnie or 'second fortress company'

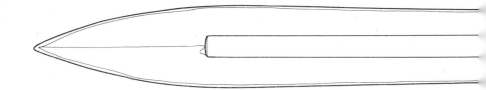

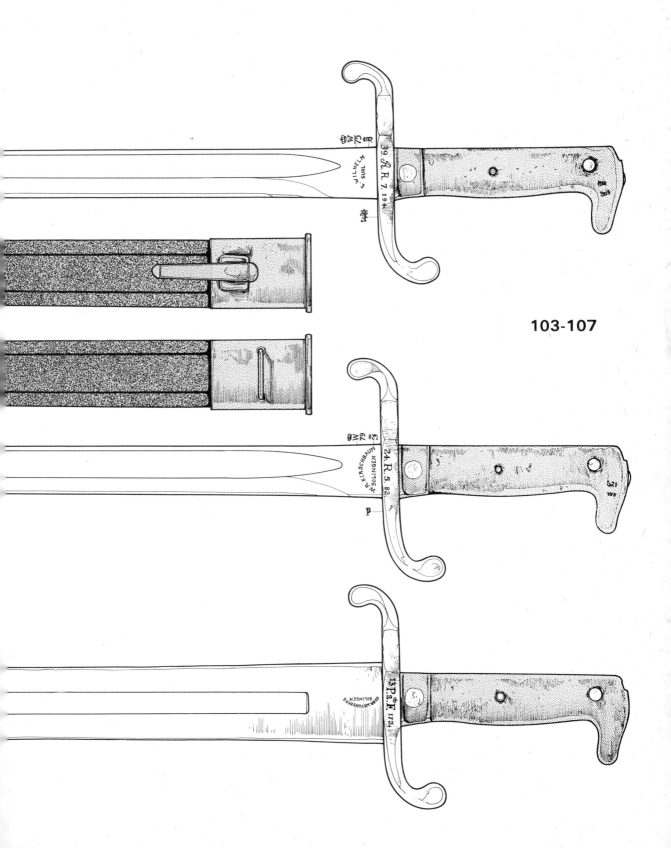

103-107

The S71 bayonets are often clearly marked with the manufacturer's name and the town of origin, while the back of the blade usually carries the monarch's cypher and the date of manufacture. Regimental markings are often found on the crossguard.

23. Pioneers' bayonets, 1871

In 1871 another bayonet with a saw-backed blade was issued to pioneer troops and designated the **Pionierfaschinenmesser 1871**. This must not be confused with the infantry saw-back previously described which was carried by NCOs. The pioneer bayonets have the same heavy brass hilt with 17 diagonal grip lines, cut into the obverse side. The other side (the reverse or left) was left plain.

The S shaped crossguard has a muzzle ring with a diameter of 17mm(0.67in). The heavy blade was designed with a saw-back so that the bayonet, when used as a tool, could do the work of saw, machète and axe—hence its weight and strength. The weight without scabbard is 822gm(29oz). It could also be used as a shortsword and as a bayonet. The blade measures 475mm(18.70in), giving the bayonet an overall length of 600mm(23.62in). The saw which runs for 350mm(13.78in) has 38 double teeth. There are two varieties, one Prussian and the other Bavarian. The model illustrated is Prussian with a true edge to the blade that reaches to within 20-25mm (0.79-1.00in) from the crossguard whereas that of Bavaria stops 127mm(5.00in) away from the guard. These were issued with broad brass-mounted black leather scabbards.

Württemberg did not follow the rest of Germany in its choice of Pionierfaschinenmesser, and instead adopted a completely different arm (though with the same hilt as the Prussian and Bavarian bayonets). They chose to keep the blade of their obsolete Pionierfaschinenmesser of 1862 which had a broad, double-edged blade slightly waisted and swelling at the point. This, the same length as the other models, has a narrow fuller centrally positioned down each side. Though it has no saw-back it could be utilised efficiently as a 'chopper' and was better in its role of shortsword and bayonet. The scabbard was again of brass-mounted leather.

Most of the bayonets carry the manufacturer's name on the blade together with the date of manufacture on the back.

All these bayonets are specialist arms issued only to pioneers, in keeping with the German principle of issuing different arms to each branch of the army. This was a common practice in contemporary Europe—Britain also had in use infantry sword and socket bayonets, as well as artillery and naval bayonets very different from each other.

24. Sword bayonet, S98 ,1898–1914

The Gewehr 98, introduced to the German army on 5th April 1898, brought with it a new concept of the way in which a bayonet could be fitted to a rifle and the result of Mauser's experimentation begun in 1894. It had been found, after a number of unsuccessful experiments, that sufficient support could be obtained from the bayonet bar (provided it was long enough) to make the muzzle ring unnecessary. One advantage of this was that the ring, whose manufacturing tolerances were on occasions critical, could be deleted from the design; this the Germans promptly did.

The standard bayonet of the Gew 98 was the **Seitengewehr 98** (S98), of which there were two dissimilar types—**aA**, *alter Art* or 'old pattern', which was manufactured in the period 1898-1902, and **nA**, *neuer Art* or 'new pattern', made from 1902 until c.1913/14. The former had a one-piece wooden grip while the latter's hilt, of a different basic shape, had two separate wood grips; in both the grip or grips were retained by two bolts of typical German type. The weakness of the one-piece grip, which often split along the underside, was responsible for the change in design: in addition, the two separate grips were easier to make. The standard infantry bayonets have slender blades of 520mm(20.47in), with pipe-backs similar in design to that of the old Hirschfänger 71 and hence to the blade of the even older Füsilier-Seitengewehr of 1860. Inspiration for all was probably provided by the British Lancaster Sappers' and Miners' carbine bayonet of 1855. The S98 has a small steel guard with a rearward swept quillon whose utility was questionable: it in any case cramps the fingers when held in the hand.

Two sawbacked versions of the S98, again of old and new pattern, were made for issue as a badge of rank to the infantry NCOs (who represented about 6% of the total establishment of an infantry regiment) and have plain blades without the swell-point or the pipe-back. A short row of double saw-teeth grace the blades' back.

The S98 bayonets were originally issued in slender steel-mounted leather scabbards, but these proved too flimsy in war and were supplemented c.1915 by issues of various all-steel types.

Many of these bayonets carry their regimental markings on the reverse sides of the guard and of the scabbard topmount, while the manufacturers' name or trademark generally appears on the ricasso together with the cypher and the date on the blade.

25.   Knife bayonet, KS98, 1901

This, usually known as the **KS98**, was the original small sawback bayonet in the German service and seems to have been produced only in the period 1901-14. The pattern was first introduced in 1901 as the weapon of the independent machine-gun formations, and its use was soon extended to airship (Luftschiffe) units. The KS98 remains, however, best known as the weapon of the machine-gunners. Many also seem to have been issued to the various components of the Kaiserliche Schutztruppen and are distinctively marked *K.S.* Others seem to have seen widespread colonial use, bearing marks such as *Sch. D.O.A.* for the Schutztruppe Deutsche Ostafrika and *Sch. K.* for the Schutztruppe Kamerun.

The bayonet itself combines some of the features of the S71/84 with some culled from the Hirschfänger of 1865 and 1871: the 250mm(9.84in) blade is sawbacked, there is an abbreviated steel guard with a rearward swept quillon, and the weapon is completed by a steel bird's head pommel. The grips on the service bayonets are of finely-chequered leather, retained to the tang by three steel rivets, but a multitude of unofficial 'dress' patterns exist with grips of rubber, horn, wood, or (in later days) plastic. It must be emphasised that these were in no way official issue and were simply purchased to the whim of the individual for wear when off-duty.

Service bayonets were issued in standard all-steel scabbards of the type later adopted for use with the S84/98.

26.   Sword bayonets, S98/05 aA and nA, 1905–1918

This bayonet is probably the most famous of the many different models used by the German armies throughout World War 1. Its designation is **Seitengewehr 98/05** (often abbreviated to S98/05): 98 for the rifle and carbine with which it was issued, and 05 for the year of its official adoption. The sawbacked version was carried by the pioneers and the plain pattern by the infantry and the foot artillery; the S98/05 was one of the few German bayonets to exist in plain and sawbacked varieties where the latter was not considered solely as NCOs issue.

The first pattern of the S98/05—later retrogressively called *alter Art*, or 'old pattern'—was adopted, as has been indicated, in 1905 although no example has yet been examined bearing a date earlier than 1907. It is thought that manufacture of the bayonet was deferred until the Kar 98 entered series production and issue, the first of which seems to have been made in 1908/9. The 'old model' is distinguished by a guard that possesses distinctive upward continuations—the result being slightly more of a muzzle ring than is found on the later 'new model'—and by the absence of the flashguard that was later found necessary to protect the back of the hilt from the muzzle flash of the Kar 98, something that otherwise charred the grips. This was not found when the bayonet was fixed to the Gew 98 simply because the full-length rifle muzzle protruded past the guard; the short muzzle of the carbine did not.

Thus it was found necessary to introduce the **S98/05 nA**, in which nA represented *neuer Art* or 'new model', distinguished by the shortened guard and the sheet-steel flashguard along the back of the grips. The drawings make this difference more clear. The new version, however, existed in both plain and sawbacked types, and was apparently introduced in 1915. It, too, has a steel guard with a rearward swept quillon, diagonally-ribbed wood grips, and a steel pommel with an internal coil-sprung press-stud. Each bayonet was produced in two basic styles, sawbacked and plain, to which a third was added c.1916/7 when many of the saws were removed by grinding: the teeth had been found virtually useless for their tasks and were nothing more than fuel for the fire of Allied propaganda—the source of many 'brutality' claims. Most grinding conversions were executed officially, and hence are often distinguished by the appearance of a small inspection stamp at the hilt end of the altered section.

It must also be noted that hybrid versions of the S98/05 exist, probably made in 1915 when the

108   Seitengewehr 98 aA, Rheinische Metallwaaren-und Maschinenfabrik, 1900; 92.Infanterie-Regiment
109   Scabbard, S98
110   Seitengewehr 98 nA sawback; V C Schilling, Suhl, 1909; 107.Infanterie-Regiment
111   Scabbard, S98, all-steel pattern c.1915
112   Scabbard, S98, all-steel pattern, 1915/16
113   Kurz Seitengewehr 98, Königlich Gewehrfabrik Erfurt, 1911; Jäger-Bataillon Nr.6
114   Seitengewehr 98/05 aA, F Herder & Sohn, Solingen, 1915
115   Scabbard, S98/05
116   Seitengewehr 98/05 nA sawback, Waffenfabrik Mauser, Oberndorf, 1917
117   Scabbard, S98/05, all-steel pattern

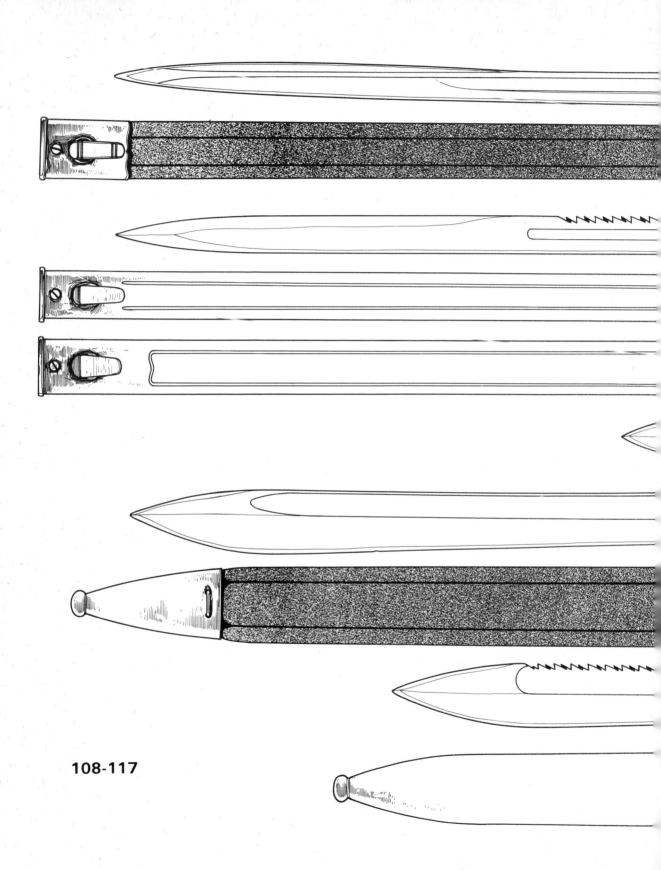

108-117

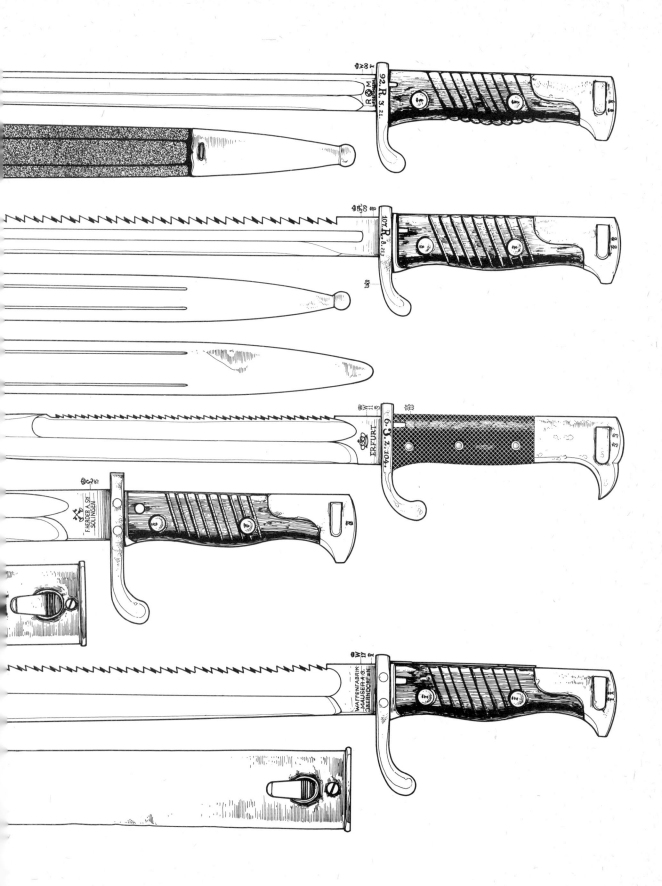

Scabbards for these bayonets, originally of steel-mounted leather, became all-steel from the introduction of the new model in 1915: in addition certain Ersatz (substitute) patterns existed in which a topmount of sheet steel was mated with a body fabricated from zinc sheeting. These scabbards, however, correctly belong to the so-called Ersatz Seitengewehr M 98/05.

As the war progressed, and Germany became increasingly short of both valuable raw material and equally-precious machine time, the manufacture of the S98/05 was discontinued (c.1917 in most cases) and a horde of all-steel bayonets of comparable pattern were made. These, **Ersatz Seitengewehre 98/05**, use hilts of steel sheet, fabricated in two sections and riveted together, with crude swell-point blades and guards incorporating the peculiar double muzzle ring that enable the bayonets to fit virtually any of the German rifles with the exception (in the cases of some other Ersatz bayonets) of the Gew 98 and Kar 98. These Ersatz S98/05 bayonets are often called Bavarian, but there is as yet no evidence to show that all were used there.

Though there were other sawbacked bayonets in the German army, none excited the attention of the Allies more than the S98/05—which caused an outcry of barbarity in the British press: it seems they had conveniently forgotten that the British artillery, engineers and infantry had been equipped just a few decades before with sawbacked swords and bayonets. By the same token the Prussian pioneers had carried combined bayonets and sawbacked sidearms since 1869.

27.   Knife bayonet, S14, 1914–1918

The **Seitengewehr 14**, or **98/14**, was not initially a standard German pattern, being instead a requisitioned type taken from stocks of bayonets that were probably intended for export to South America. Most of the originals, it is thought, were manufactured with quillons which were removed (along with the muzzle rings) for issue to the German armies; the result fitted the Gew and Kar 98. The grips are generally held by rivets set in washers, somewhat unlike the contemporary German practice of using bolts.

The S14 bayonets are without exception fitted with 300mm(11.81in) blades, although there are several different types of blade: those made by 'Bayard' (Anciens Établissements Pieper of Herstal-léz-Liège) have squared fullers, while those of the weapons made in Suhl by Samson-Werke are rounded. Similarly the shape of the pommels is

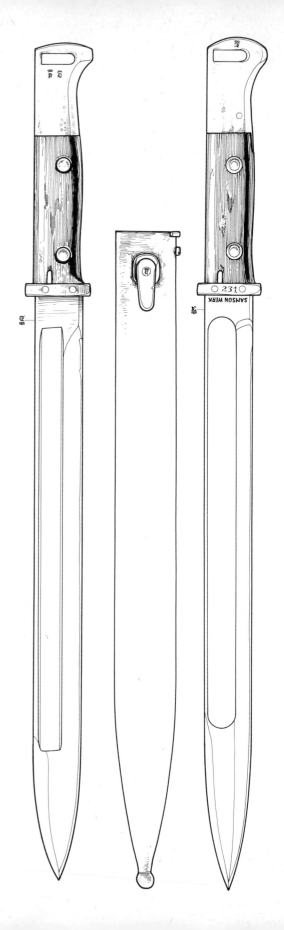

subject to some variety, and a few bayonets—probably completed after the war had begun or wartime repairs—can now be found with bolts in place of rivets. All have conventional steel hilts with wood grips and internal coil-spring press-studs, and some also have sheet-steel flashguards along the back. Others may be found with sawbacks, generally of 19 double teeth, which marks them as NCOs issue.

All were issued in all-steel scabbards of standard German pattern, with a frog-stud and the mouthpiece's blade-retaining springs secured by a small screw on the scabbard-side.

These weapons are interesting in that they used blades not initially of standard German design, but which later influenced the size of so many Ersatz types.

28. Knife bayonets, S84/98, 1915–1945

This bayonet, with its 250mm(9.84in) blade, was the shortest of the German regulation patterns to see service in World War 1 and the design continued to be used through World War 2.

The **S84/98** bayonets used in World War 1 fall into two categories: those conversions of the old S71/84, the transformation of which is thought to have occurred at the beginning of 1915, and those of new manufacture. The former are easily recognised by the distinctive blade of the earlier weapon, with square fullers—some of which run the length of the blade—and the appearance of dates in the 1880s. These were simply altered by removing the old pommels and replacing them with one suited to the Gew 98, while at the same time the muzzle ring was removed to similar purpose. These converted bayonets always have the backs of the hilt shaped to the hand, although there is reason to suspect the existence of a bayonet of similar type with a straight back and a flashguard.

The S84/98 bayonets of new manufacture were recognisable by the hilts, of steel with wood grips which were occasionally secured by rivets rather than bolts. The blades were also of different form to those of the conversions, although once again a variety exists in the way in which the blades were fullered: some have square fullers while others are gently tapered. Some bayonets have flashguards: others have

not. And some are also found with sawbacks of nineteen double teeth.

Many of these bayonets were retained through the period of the Reichswehr (1920-33), most being blued and some bearing four-figure serial numbers—generally indicative of police issue. The bayonet was then taken as that of the Wehrmacht, and manufacture again commenced c.1935 with wooden grips and standard tapered fullers. From 1937 most of the manufacturers turned to grips of plastic, varying in hue between orange and black, although some wood-gripped specimens are known bearing dates as late as 1940. A difference also exists between the flashguards of the weapons produced in World War 1, which are folded so that the edges of the guards are visible underneath the hilts, and those made in the period of the Third Reich, whose shorter guards do not protrude.

Imperial-period bayonets bear their manufacturer's marks and (occasionally) dated cyphers in typical fashion, while the later post-1935 weapons bear various S-codes or later three-letter codes, together with serial numbers, in some cases dates (usually in the form '39' for 1939) and—more rarely—a maker's name.

All were issued in all-steel scabbards, bright-finished prior to 1933/5 and blued thereafter, amongst which few differences may be noted; the Third Reich ones, however, are more tapered than the originals and have the blade-retaining spring screw on the side of the scabbard rather than on the face above the frog-stud.

Note
It has long been rumoured that a sawbacked version of the Third Reich S84/98 was issued, ostensibly for the use of the Waffen-SS. One has been examined and there is good reason to doubt its authenticity; no official documentation has ever been produced and it is thus suspected that those bayonets now available are spurious. The specimen examined bore the code *fuj* (which could not be identified and is therefore itself suspect) together with the date '43' for 1943. But if it is a fake, the standard of the workmanship of the sawback suggests that it has been professionally—if recently—altered.

29. Ersatz bayonets

By 1916, the German authorities were in desperate need of large quantities of weapons with which to

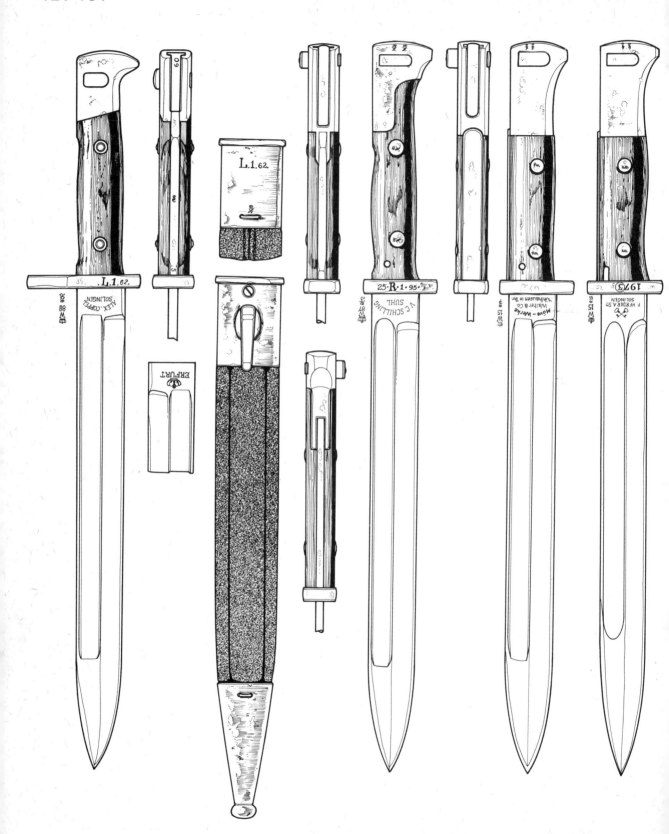

arm their troops. The country's industries were beginning to feel the shortage of raw material and machine-time, and so the production of such non-essentials as service bayonets was severely curtailed. The service weapons were complicated, and hence did not readily lend themselves to mass-production in small ill-equipped factories, so attempts were made to supplement the regular issue with simplified patterns which have come to be called *Ersatz* (German for substitute) bayonets.

There are, unfortunately, so many minor variations that it is impossible to do anything here, beyond acknowledging their existence. A catalogue of the different types is being prepared, but the work is as yet unfinished and it is not yet possible to make a definite statement of the numbers of different patterns. Most Ersatz bayonets have blades of 250mm(9.84in) or 300mm(11.81in) with hilts cast of iron or brass, and some have crossguards with 'double muzzle rings' (open at the top) which enabled them to fit the service rifles of 1871, 1884 and 1888.

Attempts were also made to embed old socket bayonet blades in Ersatz hilts, particularly old Belgian and Austro-Hungarian blades, while extensive programmes of rehilting produced hybrids using the blades from old German regulation weapons and from such things as Vetterli sword and Gras épée bayonets. Alterations, usually effected by grinding away parts of the pommel and hilt and by reaming-out or bushing muzzle rings, were made to French Mle 66 and Mle 74 bayonets, and the result was a large supply of serviceable, if obsolete, bayonets which could be issued to second line and home-garrison troops to release supplies of better weapons for the front.

Hungary

30.   Sword bayonet, 1935

In 1935 Hungary adopted a new rifle of Mannlicher design in 8mm calibre. During World War 2 the 35M (model 1935) was manufactured for the Germans and redesignated the Gewehr 98/40, after the calibre had been altered to 7.92mm, and the magazine redesigned to take the rimless cartridge. This weapon, with small modifications, was then adopted by the Hungarians as the 43M rifle.

The bayonets issued with these arms are very distinctive and very different from contemporary developments in other European countries. French nineteenth-century influence is evident, particularly from the Modèle 1886 épée bayonet for the Lebel rifle.

The Hungarian bayonets all have 370mm(13in) cruciform blades. These, designed as double-edged knife blades, have two raised strengthening ribs: one on either side. The steel hilts have a 15mm muzzle ring with a press-stud similar to that of the Lebel, which operates a catch in the base of the muzzle ring. The cylindrical wood grip slides over the bayonet tang and is held in place by the pommel. This grip has a flat panel on each side. The round pommel has a central hole leading into the hollow tang and this fits over a protruding stud on the nosecap of the rifle.

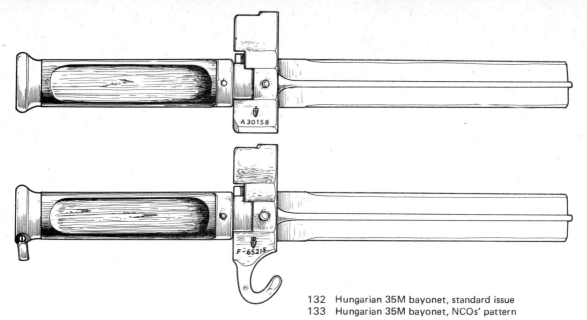

The overall length of the bayonet is 479mm(18.5in). The scabbards are plain steel, painted olive green, with typical Hungarian frog-studs and leather frogs identical to those used on the Austro-Hungarian Modell 1895 bayonets.

The first type manufactured in Budapest (by Fémaru-Fegyver és Gépgyár—FGGY) has a plain muzzle ring and the second pattern has a foresight, a practice again typically Austro-Hungarian. This raised foresight compensated for the necessary alteration in aim caused by the addition of a fixed bayonet, which interfered with the barrel vibrations and thus the flight of the bullet. The earlier type has a much deeper hole in the pommel than the later models. The old Austro-Hungarian practice of issuing NCOs with a modified bayonet was continued: these have a small upturned quillon and a swivel on the pommel to take a bayonet knot in the national colours of green, white and red.

During the last war many Hungarian troops serving alongside the German Wehrmacht were issued with the old Modell 1895 rifles and bayonets; this, together with the short period in which 35M bayonets and rifles were made, accounts for their great scarcity. They are stamped with the Hungarian arms displayed on a shield surmounted by a crown, together with a single letter and a five figure serial number on the crossguard.

India

31. India Pattern bayonets, 1907–1945

Under British rule, India manufactured large quantities of British-designed weapons for the use of the resident British troops and the large native army. When the SMLE rifle was adopted in Britain, together with the Pattern 1907 bayonet, the weapons were produced from September of 1907 in the Rifle Factory at Ishapore (RFI). The first bayonets made at Ishapore had the sweptforward quillon declared obsolete in 1913 by an order which discontinued the production of quilloned bayonets, and required that all such bayonets then held in store or in issue should be modified when the opportunity presented itself: fortunately some have survived intact. A cleaning hole was drilled through the pommel during World

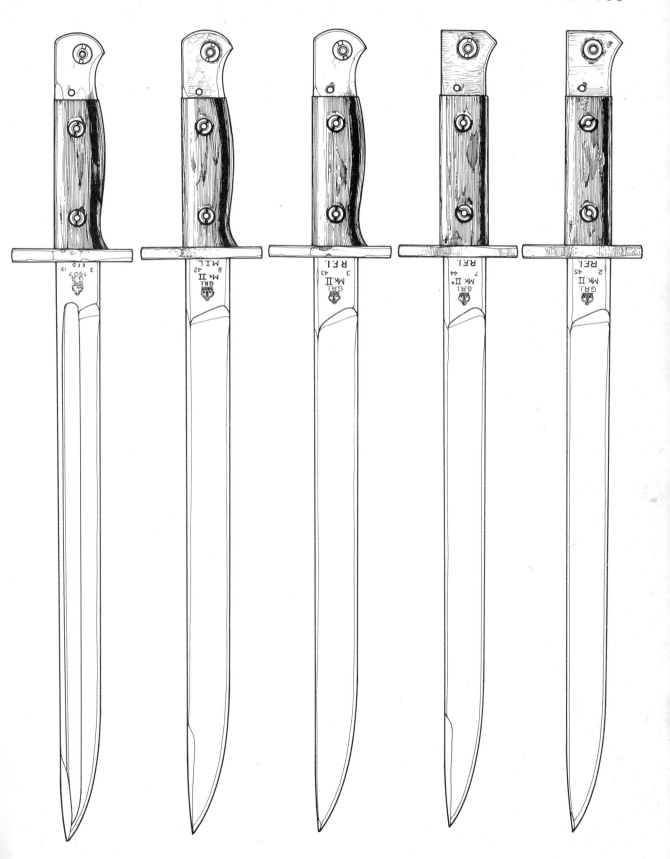

War 1, an innovation introduced by RFI in 1917 following a directive originally issued in January 1916. Production continued into the early 1920s, ceased for a while, and began again in 1940.

All the Indian bayonets are clearly marked on the blades with the date of manufacture, the factory's initials *R.F.I.*, the pattern date (1907), and the Imperial crown over *G.R.I.* for Georgius Rex Imperator. The reverse side bears the Indian government inspector's stamp of *GR* together with the Indian broad arrow over *I*.

The P07 was redesignated Bayonet No 1 Mk 1 in 1926. At the outbreak of war in 1939 arms were needed for the expanding armies, and so production of the No 1 Mk 1 was recommenced at RFI and the full 432mm(17.00in) blade was retained until 1941. By late 1941 India alone had decided to produce a shorter bayonet, probably because the long-bladed Mk 1 was found to be too long and unwieldy for jungle warfare, and so some of the Mk 1 bayonets had their blades shortened to 305mm(12.00in). A short false-edge was added to the back of the blades, which were stamped with the date of conversion and the Indian designation Mk 1*.

There is considerable confusion over the designations of all the short bayonets produced in India during the war, the principal reason for which is that they were redesignated on more than one occasion. All were ultimately classified (after 1947) as of Mk 2 type, but it is apparent that while the bayonets were being redesignated the instructions to mark them thus were not followed by some of the manufacturers. Furthermore, while the postwar Indian army has classified them all as Mk 2, the postwar Pakistani army has evidently retained the earlier designations Mk 1*, Mk 2, Mk 2*, Mk 3 and Mk 3*. With the exception of the modified Mk 1 bayonets (the Mk 1*) the remaining short bayonets will be referred to as of Mk 2 pattern.

By 1942 the first Mk 2 bayonets were put into production at RFI and at other firms who had converted to arms production. These weapons retained the Mk 1 hilt but utilised a new 305mm(12.00in) blade, without any fullers and with a short false-edge at the point. A few were stamped *Mk.1** and overstamped *Mk.II*. Some were also marked as of Mk 2* type, which is also the postwar Pakistani designation.

As production requirements increased so the false-edge was eliminated, though there was again no definite change in production: some were made with the false-edge and others at the same time without it. These bayonets were usually stamped *Mk. II*, although *Mk.II** occasionally appeared. The designation Mk 2 was applied to these weapons by the postwar Pakistani army.

The next major change in design of the Mk 2 bayonets was again introduced to accelerate production, by leaving the pommel square and by making the grips with parallel sides. This also solved the problems of grip replacement, as one grip would fit either side of the hilt: this avoided the necessity to have paired grips, one for each side. The emergency pattern again appeared with and without the false edge, but from the start of manufacture some bayonets were made *with* it. The Pakistani designations are Mk 3 (without the edge) and Mk 3* (with the edge). In practice the majority made between 1943 and 1945 was stamped *Mk.II*, though some may be found marked *Mk.II** or *Mk.III*. All of the 'Mk 2' bayonets described above have the *IS* (India Stores) inspection mark on their blades.

Though there is such confusion concerning the markings, the redesignations often ignored by those making the weapons, and the differences in the postwar classifications used in India and in Pakistan, the most convenient solution seems to be to call the original No 1 Mk 1 (P07) just that, the shortened conversion the **Sword Bayonet No 1 Mk 1***, and all the remainder **Sword Bayonets No 1 Mk 2 first pattern** (with the unaltered hilt) or **No 1 Mk 2 second pattern** ('squared' hilts): the qualification 'with/without false-edge' can then be made.

The Rifle Factory at Ishapore (RFI) produced the bulk of the Indian bayonets and, though some were made by small factories, the bulk of the remainder were produced either by the Moghulpura Workshop of the North Western Railway (blades stamped *N.W.R.*), situated at Lahore in the Punjab, or by Metal Industries Lahore (*M.I.L.*).

During the war most bayonets' hilts were painted khaki, with the blades left bright. The 'old pattern' long scabbards were issued until after the war, when the opportunity was taken of shortening the majority to fit the 305mm(12.00in) blades.

Italy

32. Sword and knife bayonets, regulation patterns, 1870–1915

In 1870 Italy adopted the Swiss-designed Vetterli rifle as the Fucile di Fanteria Modello 70, and with it a sword bayonet — the **Sciabola Baionetta Modello 70** — which remained unaltered for seventeen years. The bayonet has a 518mm(20.37in) blade with deep fullers and a conventional steel hilt employing a press stud operated by a long leaf spring on the obverse (or right) side of the pommel. The sweptforward quillon ends in a round finial and the muzzle ring is of 17.5mm(0.689in) diameter. The first Vetterli bayonets had polished composition grips, but these were found to be too fragile and were replaced at a later date with wooden ones when the bayonets were returned for repairs (probably after the turn of the century).

The very long leaf spring is held in place by the grip-retaining bolt nearest the crossguard, while the second grip bolt is inset in the grips below the leaf spring and is hence visible only on the reverse or left side of the weapon. The bayonets' overall length is 646mm(25.40in) and they were issued in brass-mounted black leather scabbards. The first pattern has long mounts and a round frog stud, while the second type — which was made in far greater numbers — has small mounts and an oval stud.

When the Vetterli rifle was modified in 1887 by the addition of a box magazine designed by Giuseppe Vitali, the bayonet design of 1870 was retained with but minor modifications. The result was the **Sciabola-Baionetta Modello 70/87,** issued with the Fucile di Fanteria Modello 70/87: a small cut-out was made in the base of the muzzle ring c.1875, but this was introduced before the Modello 70/87 . It was also found expedient to replace the long leaf spring with a shorter one attached by means of the grip bolt nearest the pommel, but in all other respects the two patterns were identical.

Most of the sword bayonets are stamped on the crossguard with a serial number, generally of two letters followed by a four-figure number. The blades are often stamped with either the name or an abbreviation of the manufacturing arsenal — thus *Torre Annunziata* for Fabbrica d'Armi Torre Annunziata, or the abbreviation *TA*. Other manufac-

turers included Fabbrica d'Armi Terni (*Terni* or *T*) and Fabbrica dell'Armi Torino (*Torino* or *TO*). The scabbard leathers are usually marked with the manufacturer and the date, for example *Brescia 1885*. 1871 also saw the introduction of the Moschetto Modello 70 da Truppe Speciali (*ie* 'for special troops'), a firearm whose length represented an intermediate stage between the rifle and the carbine. The Moschetto was issued with a sword bayonet whose hilt was the same as that of the standard rifle bayonet, but which was mated with a cruciform blade some 277mm(11.00in) long. This, the **Sciabola-Baionetta da Truppe Speciali Modello 70,** was issued with a tapering leather scabbard with brass mounts.

During World War 1, some bayonets — including Modello 70 and Modello 70/87 — were shortened until the blade length was some 235mm(9.25in). The blade tips were then taken to make emergency bayonets to which all-metal hilts were attached. The quillons were also removed from the sword patterns, and the scabbards were modified to suit the reduced size. The resulting bayonets, usually known as the **Sciabola-Baionetta (accorciata) Modello 70/87/15,** were issued to the troops armed with old modello 70/87 rifles whose barrels had been bored out and then fitted with a 6.5mm calibre liner, with which they could fire the standard 6.5mm cartridges used with the rifle pattern of 1891. The M70/87/15 was issued only to the Milizia Mobile.

Another variety of the Vetterli sword bayonets exists in which the blades have been shortened to 310-320mm(12.25-12.50in) and their scabbards similarly altered to 335mm(13.25in). The muzzle rings have been bushed to about 16mm(0.630in), but it is not known with certainty for which rifles this was executed.

Note
A sword bayonet is also known to exist for the Fucile da Marina modello 1882 (the so-called Vetterli-Bertoldo). No specimen of this bayonet has yet been discovered, but it is thought to combine the hilt of the modello 70 bayonet with a recurved guard to which an abbreviated handguard is fitted. It is assumed that a brass-mounted leather scabbard is used, and that the bayonet's dimensions are roughly comparable to those of the modello 70.

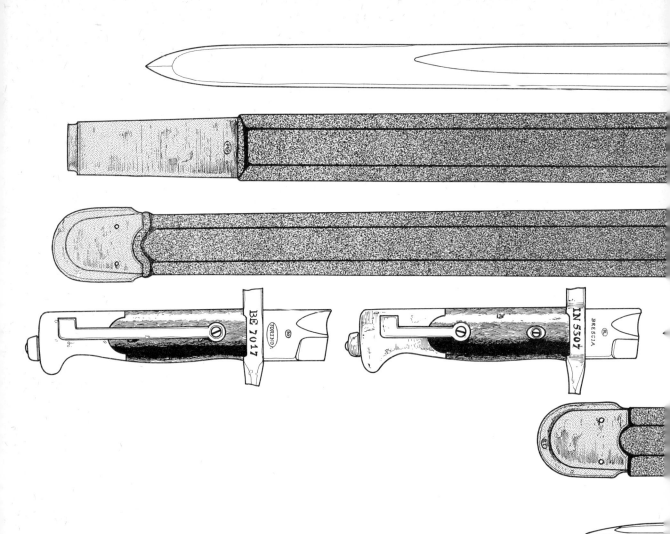

139   Sciabola-baionetta M70, number BE7017, made by Fabbrica d'Armi Torino
140   Scabbard, M70, first pattern with long mounts, pre c.1875
141   Scabbard, M70, second pattern, marked 'Terni 1886'
142   Obverse hilt and ricasso of 139
143   Sciabola-baionetta M70/87, number IN5307, by Fabbrica d'Armi Brescia
144   Sciabola-baionetta M70/87, number AE3533, made by Fabbrica d'Armi Torre Annunziata and shortened c.1915
145   The obverse guard and ricasso of 144
146   Scabbard, M70, shortened in c.1915; back marked 'Brescia 1880'
147   Sciabola-baionetta M70 TS, probably made by Fabbrica d'Armi Torino
148   Sciabola-baionetta 'M70/91', number 4330, a conversion of an M70 blade to fit the Fucile M91

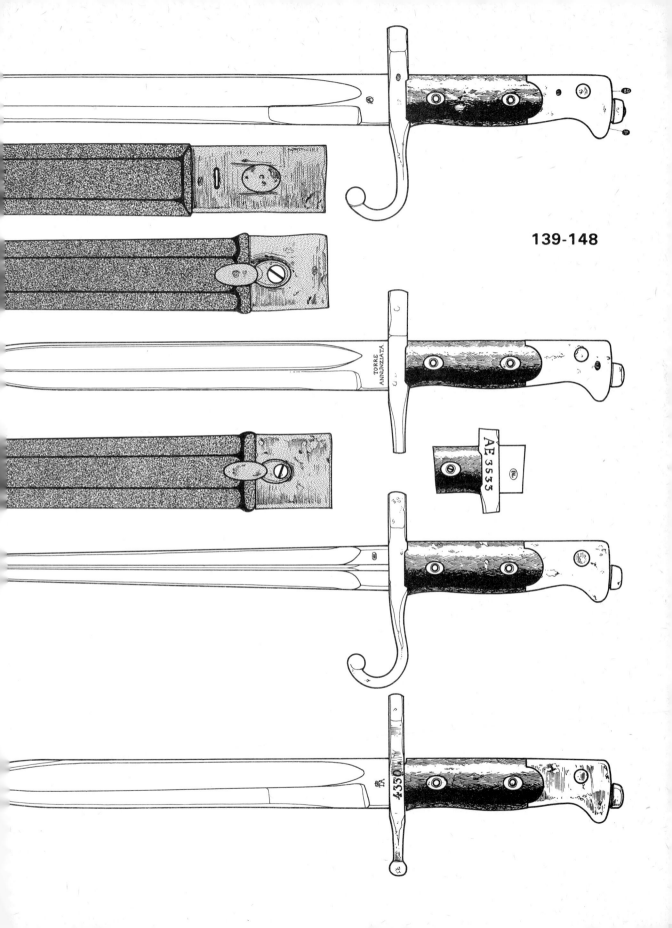

139-148

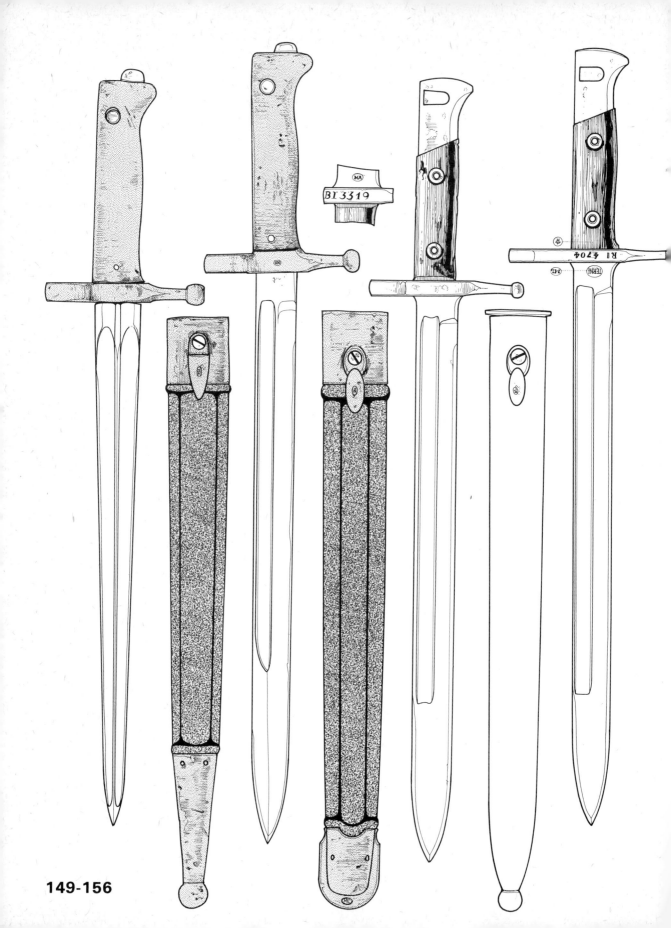

149-156

33. Sword and knife bayonets, emergency patterns, 1915–1918

Italy, in common with most of the combatants, was forced to reissue obsolete arms to her hard-pressed troops to supplement the stocks of modern weapons. The struggle against the forces of Austria-Hungary called for more and more men and arms, until the disaster of Caporetto forced the defending Italians to send every able-bodied man and every serviceable weapon into the war. The old Modello 70/87 rifles were brought out of storage, and some were promptly modified to handle the 6.5mm cartridge used with the rifles and carbines of the Modello 91 system. The alteration to the Vetterli guns was achieved by boring out the existing rifling and then inserting a rifled sub-calibre liner into the barrel; a new box magazine was added to the action, and the result was a serviceable rifle that was issued to the Milizia Mobile. Though many of these rifles were issued with the shortened modello 70/87 sword bayonets (the results being known as the Modello 70/87/15), some were issued with a modified pattern of the standard modello 91 sword bayonet known as the **Sciabola-Baionetta Modello 70/87/91/15** or the **Modello 87/91/15**.

This bayonet is identical to the standard 1891 pattern with a steel hilt, plain wood grips, a small straight quillon, a single-edged 300mm (11.81in) blade and a steel-mounted leather scabbard. The muzzle ring is, however, placed close to the back of the hilt and has a diameter of 17.5mm (0.689in) to fit over the larger barrel of the Vetterli rifle. The position and diameter of the ring are the only features that distinguish this bayonet from the standard modello 91. The rifle's bayonet bar was modified by cutting a notch in the top side of the attachment lug, owing to the fact that the press-stud mechanism of the Modello 91 is on the opposite side to that of the Modello 70 and Modello 70/87 bayonets.

Another bayonet manufactured for the converted Vetterli rifles has a solid cast-brass hilt, a short straight quillon with a large ball terminal and the same 300mm (11.81in) blade. The crossguard, containing a standard 17.5mm (0.689in) muzzle ring is cast as an integral part of the grip. The blade tang passes through the hilt to be secured by a steel stud at the end of the pommel. This bayonet's press-stud follows the old Vetterli pattern by placing it on the reverse or left side of the hilt. It is operated by a long (90mm/3.50in) leaf spring. The serial number is stamped on the crossguard, and the scabbard was any of the patterns described under the Modello 91. Quite what the Italians called this particular bayonet is a little mysterious, but is is suggested that the term **Modello 70/87/16** could have been used to differentiate between this pattern and the Modello 70/87/15 — which was a shortened version of the old full-length bayonets.

An emergency bayonet was also made for the Moschetto da Truppe Speciali Modello 70/87/15, another of the conversions to handle the 6.5mm cartridge. This bayonet, apparently known as the **Sciabola Baionetta Modello 70/87/16 da Moschetto** used a cast-brass hilt with an integral muzzle ring and quillon and was fitted with the cruciform blade of the old Modello 70 Truppe Speciali bayonet.

34. Knife bayonets, 1891–1918

Italy officially adopted the Fucile di Fanteria Modello 91 on 29th March 1892, and the rifle became the standard weapon of the line infantry through both wars (although in World War 2 it was supplemented by the Modello 91/38). The bayonet, known as the **Sciabola-Baionetta Modello 91**, remained issue throughout the period.

The bayonet has a single-edged blade some 300mm (11.81in) long, with a spear point and deep square-ended fullers on both sides of the blade. The hilt has a straight crossguard with a small ball finial on the tip of the quillon and a muzzle ring of 13mm (0.512in) diameter. The plain wood grips, which meet the pommel diagonally, are held in place by two steel rivets set into washers. The pommel is conventional with a T-groove and an internal coil-spring press-stud. The overall length of the weapon is some 412mm (16.20in), and it was issued with all the steel parts in a heavily blued condition.

Four patterns of scabbard were made for this bayonet. The first, typically Italian, has a black leather body with mounts of brass: the second differed only in the material of the mounts, which was changed to steel. The third type was made

149 Sciabola-baionetta M70/87/16 TS
150 Scabbard, M70 TS
151 Sciabola-baionetta M70/87/16, number KZ2905, using an M91 blade
152 Obverse guard and ricasso
153 Scabbard, M91, marked 'ARET 1914' on the back
154 Sciabola-baionetta M87/91/15, number B13133, basically an M91 to fit the M70/87 rifle
155 Scabbard, M91, steel
156 Sciabola-baionetta M91, number R14704, made by Fabbrica d'Armi Terni

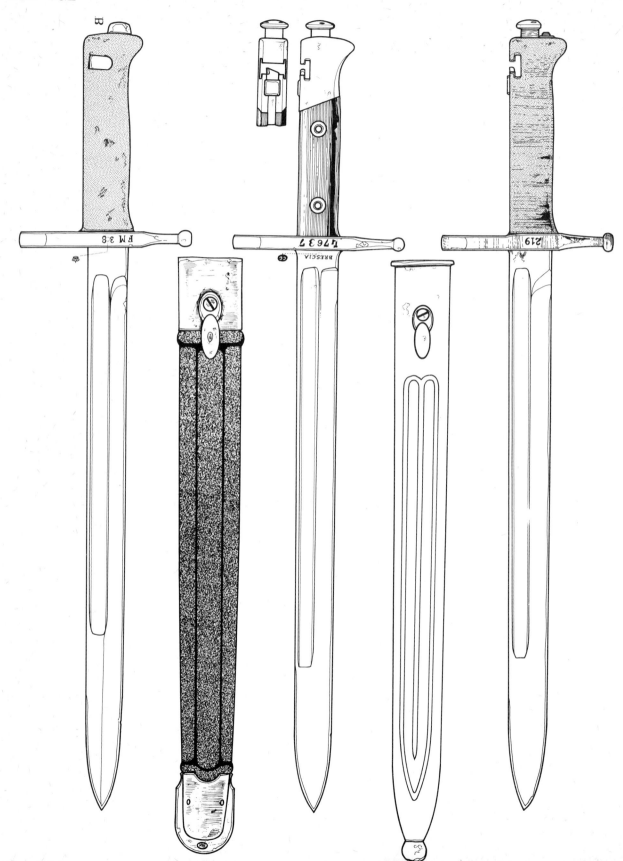

entirely of steel with a raised pattern which was apparently added for no other purpose than to obtain a decorative appearance. The fourth scabbard, again of steel, was entirely plain: this type, made in very limited numbers, is often confused with the plain steel scabbards used by the Austrians for captured Italian bayonets. The frog stud on the latter, however, is very typically Austro-Hungarian.

During World War 1 a variation of the Modello 91 was made in which the steel pommel and wood grips were replaced by a plain hilt of cast-brass, although the crossguard remained the standard steel pattern. These bayonets, apparently known as the **Sciabola-Baionetta Modello 91/16**, are very rare and are also occasionally found with the hilt painted black. The blade tang passes through the brass hilt and is hammered tight at the pommel, where it also passes through a round steel stud. The brass-mounted leather scabbard is correct for this pattern of bayonet.

A variation of the Modello 91 bayonet was also made for the Moschetto Modello 91 per Truppe Speciali, introduced in 1897, in which the method of attaching the bayonet was completely changed. The Modello 91 TS bayonet (the **Sciabola-Baionetta Modello 91 da Moschetto per Truppe Speciali**) is identical in all but the lock mechanism to the standard Modello 91, but a T-groove is cut across the pommel and the press-stud protrudes from the pommel's end. Quite why the Italians thought it necessary to introduce a lock of this type is a mystery, but it is suggested that this was one way in which a bayonet could not be dislodged from the carbine's barrel by a direct pull: it also, in theory at least, prevents undue strain on the lock mechanism (especially the lock surface) which otherwise occurred when the soldier was—for example—thrusting the bayonet into an enemy!

The Modello 91 TS bayonet, together with the brass-hilted **Sciabola-Baionetta Modello 91/16 TS** (identical to the Modello 91/16 described above, with the exception of the lock mechanism), was issued with the brass-mounted leather scabbard.

Most of the four patterns of Modello 91 bayonet are marked on the crossguard with a serial number and on the blade with the place of manufacture. The leather scabbards are usually stamped with the place and date of manufacture on the back, running down-

wards alongside the seam. Thus a Modello 91 bayonet might bear the serial number *A5569* on the guard, the mark *Terni* on the blade, and *A.C.T.1916* on the scabbard.

In addition to the standard Modello 91 bayonets, a version of the old Vetterli sword bayonet was also adapted in small numbers for the Modello 91 rifle: the alteration consisted of shortening the Vetterli blade to about 300mm(11.81in) and discarding the old crossguards in favour of that of the standard Modello 91. This particular bayonet, probably known as the **Sciabola-Baionetta Modello 71/91**, is especially rare.

35.   Knife bayonets, folding and fixed blade types, 1938–1945

The story of these weapons is a little confused; very little, for example, has been found in print either to confirm their chronology or to confirm whether the submachine-gun bayonet preceded the rifle design (or whether the reverse was the case).

In the absence of confirmatory information, it is suggested that the first of the Italian folding bayonets appeared c.1936 with the Moschetto Semiautomatico Beretta Modello 35, the prototype for the later Modello 38A submachine-gun. This bayonet, apparently made in very small quantities, had neither ring nor crossguard; instead, reminiscent of German practice, it was attached solely by the support afforted by the T-lug engaging with the pommel groove. An unusual locking catch was placed beneath the pommel where it operated the locking mechanism within the groove; this method, however, proved unsatisfactory and some of these bayonets are known in which the latch-lock of the 'first pattern' Modello 91/38 folding bayonet replaced the pommel catch. The blade of the MSB 35 bayonet was longer than that of the standard rifle bayonets, approximately 196mm (7.75in), but in spite of the increased length it would still fit in the standard scabbard.

In January 1938 the Italian army adopted the Beretta submachine gun as the Moschetto Automatico Beretta Modello 38A (MAB 38A), and with it an improved folding bayonet which—it is thought—inspired the development of the Modello 91/38 rifle type. This was fitted with a latch-lock and a T-lug where the muzzle ring was normally placed: this mated with a slot cut into the front of the barrel casing. The latch-lock was found to be both difficult to operate and fragile, and so the second pattern of Modello 38 bayonet—the **Baionetta da Moschetto con lama ripiegabile Modello 38**—was given a standard press-stud. The submachine-gun bayonets are now relatively rare and were only made in the period 1938-9, after which the idea of mounting a bayonet on the Beretta was abandoned.

The Italians had realised from their 1936 campaigns in Ethiopia that their 6.5mm cartridge was not as lethal as some of those current in other armies—the 7.9mm Mauser and the 0.303in, for example—and so their ordnance authorities introduced a 7.35mm round, basically an enlarged-mouth version of the 6.5mm type, in which it was hoped to eliminate the problems. First issues of the new cartridge, together with the Fucile di Fanteria Modello 91/38 (sometimes called Modello 38), were made in 1938, but the onset of World War 2 caused the Italians to revert to their 6.5mm cartridge before universal issue of the larger-calibre weapons had been made. Hence, for the duration of the war, the two calibres and the various rifles and carbines of Modello 38 type—most of which could be found chambered for either round—were issued together. The Italian ordnance, especially where ammunition was concerned, rarely showed much appreciation of logistics.

Thus some of the Italian trooops carried the Modello 91/38 rifles together with the various Modello 91/38 knife bayonets. The first was a peculiar little weapon with a blade that could be folded back into the grip, to be used when the bayonet was fixed to the rifle but not in use; the blade point, which protruded past the grips, was contained within a slot cut into the rifle's fore end. The weapon was called the **Baionetta con lama ripiegabile Modello 91/38,** literally the 'bayonet with folding blade', and was normally carried in a standard scabbard fixed to the soldier's belt. The single-edged knife blade was 175mm (6.87in) long and was locked by means of a press-stud in the crossguard; this was pushed to disengage the lock, whereupon the blade

could be swung downwards and back into the slot cut into the hilt. There it was locked in position by the engagement of the press-stud with the heel of the blade. The attachment to the rifle was effected by a standard muzzle ring (of 13mm/0.512in diameter), a T-groove on the pommel and a standard pommel-mounted press-stud. The first Modello 91/38 bayonets were, however, fitted with an unusual laterally-swinging latch-lock (and called **Baionetta con lama ripiegabile e leva di svincolo Modello 91/38**—or 'bayonet with folding blade and locking lever'), but the latch—which was pivoted in the middle and had a grooved thumbpiece—was found to be fragile and clumsy; it was then replaced, after c.1939, by the well-tried and reliable press-stud. The hilts of both patterns had plain wood grips secured by two small slotted-head bolts set in steel washers. The metal surfaces were blued.

The folding bayonets were found to be insufficiently strong for field use, and introduced needless complication to a military weapon that had to be strong and as simple as possible. During the war, therefore, the bayonets were manufactured without the press-stud on the guard and with a short fixed quillon. This effectively locked the bayonet firmly in the open position without altering any other parts, and c.1942/3 a further change was made by discarding the concept of a folding bayonet entirely and instead making the Modello 91/38 a true knife bayonet. In the latter case the hilt is solid with wood grips riveted to the tang and a crossguard without the rearward catch housing was fitted, although the bayonet retained the overall dimensions of the earlier patterns. Both patterns, the 'altered fixed' and the newly-made knife types, were apparently known as the **Baionetta con lama fissa Modello 91/38** (ie 'with fixed blade') to distinguish them from the folding-blade weapons.

Most of these bayonets have their serial numbers on their crossguard, together with the manufacturers' name or trademark along the back of the hilt. Two types of scabbard exist, both of which are sufficiently long to take both the rifle bayonet and the longer-bladed submachine-gun pattern. Both have blued steel bodies, but one has a frog stud and the other a diagonal steel loop.

163 Baionetta M38, latch-lock pattern, folded; the number 1213 denotes Finnish use
164 Baionetta M91/38, latch-lock type, number 194960
165 Baionetta M38, press-stud type, with Finnish number 7403
166 Scabbard, M38 type 1
167 Baionetta M91/38, press-stud type, number A78766
168 Scabbard, M38 type 2
169 Baionetta M91/38, fixed-blade type made from old parts; numbered 160150 (original) and Y6817
170 Scabbard, M38 type 3
171 Baionetta M91/38, new manufacture with fixed guard, number G68736
172 Scabbard, M38; this is a Finnish type
173 Scabbard, M38; this is a Finnish type

163-173

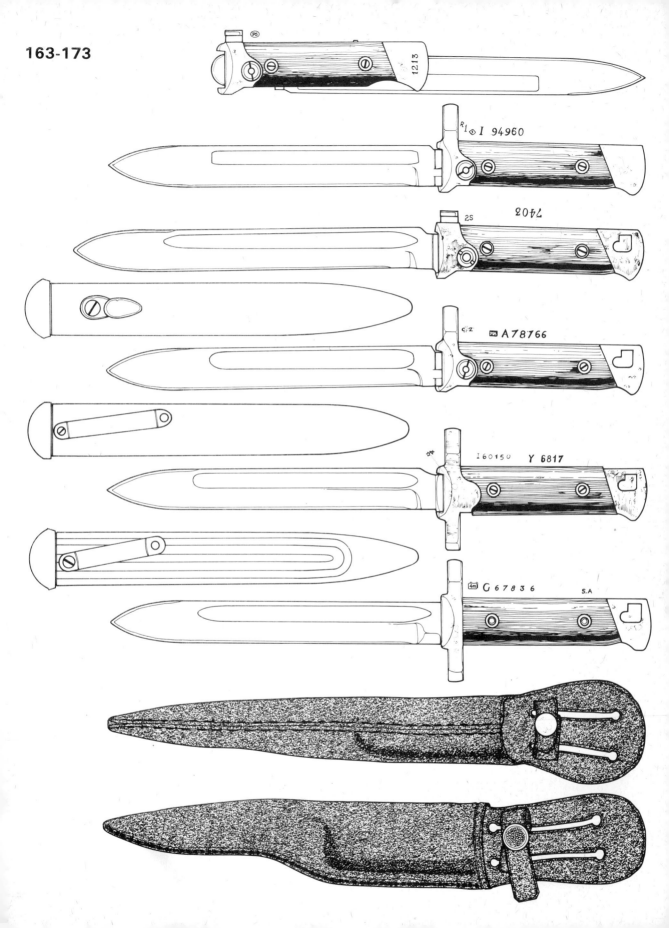

Note

In addition to the standard types of submachine-gun bayonet, guns made to contracts (for the Moschetto Automatico Beretta Modello 38/49) placed in 1949 by Egypt used the standard Modello 91/38 rifle bayonets, in which case the muzzle ring was placed around the front part of the compensator. These folding bayonets were readily available from surplus stock, and it is possible that guns manufactured to other contracts placed and fulfilled in the same era were similarly equipped.

Japan

36. Sword and knife bayonets, 1897–1945

The experiences of the Japanese army in the Sino-Japanese war of 1894, together with the advances made in contemporary European weapons design, convinced the Japanese ordnance authorities that their Murata repeating rifle was obsolete. A board was convened at the Tokyo explosives factory, headed by Murata, and by late 1895 the design of a 6.5mm cartridge had been completed. A second board (headed by Colonel Nariake Arisaka) was then ordered to investigate rifle design, and the result was the introduction in March 1897 of the 30th year infantry rifle and the 30th year carbine; Japanese terminology is sometimes a little confusing, based as it usually was on the years of the emperor's reign, and in this case the thirtieth year was that of the reign of emperor Meiji (1868-1912). Thus the rifle was introduced in 1897, the year 1868 having been taken as year 1, and its design leaned heavily on the ideas of Mauser and Mannlicher.

Together with the rifle the Japanese adopted a new bayonet to replace the small 20th year (Murata) pattern of 1887; the **30th year bayonet**—usually wrongly called the M1897 in Western terms—heavily influenced the later British Pattern 1907, and had a sword blade of 395mm(15.55in) with a single edge that curved upwards at the point to meet the straight back. The guard, with a graceful sweptforward quillon, was of steel and had a muzzle ring with the small diameter of 14mm(0.551mm) while the wood grips were secured to the tang by two bolts set in oval-head washers of distinctive appearance. The pommel met the grips diagonally and was of steel, with a conventional T-type bar attachment groove and an internal coil-spring press-stud mechanism.

The 30th year bayonets are well made of good materials and are, in their original state, excellently finished of a deep lustrous blue. Most, however, saw hard use in World War 2 and are thus now in poor condition. In World War 1 the British acquired a large number of Arisaka rifles—perhaps as many as 200000—from the Japanese, and issued them together with their bayonets to the navy and to training depots: this meant that supplies of the Lee-Enfield type rifles could be released for service in the trenches. The British designation for the bayonet seems to have been the Pattern 1900 or **Sword Bayonet, 0.256in Rifle, P/1900**; by the same token the rifles were known as the *Rifle, Magazine, 0.256in Pattern 1900* (30th year rifle), and the *Magazine Rifle and Carbine, 0.256in, Pattern 1907* (38th year rifle and carbine). Most were stamped with British regimental stamps and serial numbers, the latter often appearing across the end of the pommel, but a lot of the British-purchased Arisaka rifles were shipped in 1916-17 to Tsarist Russia, where many were issued to the Czechoslovak Legion: 128000 Arisaka rifles were supplied from Britain to Russia, together with 600000 others supplied directly from Japan. The Russian-used 30th year bayonets are rarely marked with anything other than the original Japanese or British arsenal and serial marks, but the frogs are occasionally found marked with cyrillic characters. The revolutionary government of Mexico also purchased a small quantity of Arisaka 38th year rifles in 1910, but these were chambered for the 7mm Mauser cartridge and were modified to take the Mexican M95 knife bayonet; the Mexicans did not take delivery of all the rifles they had ordered, and so the Japanese supplied 35400 of them to the Russians in 1915—but just what bayonets these weapons used is open to considerable doubt!

The 30th year bayonets lasted a long time in the Japanese service: in 1902 a modified rifle, the 35th year naval rifle, was introduced together with the **35th year bayonet**—which was no more than a standard 30th year type modified by the addition of a catch to hold the bayonet in the scabbard. This was placed on the back of the grips and protruded through the crossguard below the muzzle ring, where it could clip over the rim of the scabbard's mouthpiece. The 30th year bayonet was also used by the 38th year rifles and carbines of 1905, but the 44th year cavalry carbine (1911) was fitted with an unusual folding bayonet attached to its nosecap.

The experiences in Manchuria, in the 1930s, showed the Japanese that they needed a larger-calibre and heavier bullet with a better ballistic performance at long ranges. The result was the Type 99 rifle and cartridge of 1939, the designation of which used a different system of nomenclature based on the founding of the Japanese imperial dynasty in 660 BC: 1939, therefore was year 2599 on the calendar. The Type 99 rifle continued to use the well-tried 30th year bayonet, which was manufactured in its quilloned form until 1941.

The onset of World War 2, with its ever-increasing grip on the supplies to the Japanese of raw materials, began a steady decline in the quality of Japanese smallarms manufacture. The bayonets, being the least important of the weapons, fared worst; indeed, they most clearly showed the effect of the cumulative shortages. Initially the quilloned guard was discontinued in favour of a straight one, the grips were then roughly finished and the pommel riveted to the tang instead of brazed, the grips became parallel-sided, the fullers were eliminated from the blade, and the design of the press-stud mechanism was simplified: the bayonet ultimately took on a form of crudity, with an ill-finished and badly tempered blade of the lowest grades of steel.

The deterioration of the bayonet was mirrored by the change in the scabbard, at first an all-steel pattern tapering at the tip to a small ball finial and with a frog-loop to receive the frog's strap, which declined to a point where it was made of laminated plywood—suitably hollowed to receive the bayonet, with crude tinplate or thin-gauge sheet steel mounts and bound with cord to provide extra strength.

The Japanese frogs were of leather with a strap and buckle, and were usually of good workmanship. Shortages of leather in wartime Japan led to the adoption of a frog made of a plastic material and some were even produced of a form of pressed cardboard, which was given a coat of clear varnish that acted as a waterproofing: some Japanese marines were issued, after c.1942/3, with a rubber frog which was moulded as an integral part of the rubber scabbard cover (inside which was either a standard steel scabbard or a wooden former).

Other Arisaka-type bayonets can also be found: the oldest is the bayonet of the Siamese Arisaka rifle of 1908, known in Siam as the Type 51: the native chronology, the Putta Sakarat era, began in 543 BC and hence the '51' in the designation referred to the year 2451 PS. The Siamese rifles and bayonets were made at the Tokyo arsenal. The **Type 51** bayonets are easily recognisable, for although having a hilt very similar to that of the 30th year Arisaka pattern the muzzle ring diameter is about 15.4mm(0.606in) and the blade is a mere 300mm(11.81in) long. The blade also ends in a centred point, compared to the back-point of the 30th year weapon. The Type 51 bayonet also usually possesses a five-figure serial number (in Siamese script) across the end of the pommel. The scabbard has a frog-stud rather than the Japanese-style loop.

The Japanese **Type 100** bayonet was a derivative of the 30th year model, intended for issue with the Type 100 submachine-gun of 1940 in which an auxiliary bayonet bar was fitted under the front of the barrel jacket: the Japanese are also known to have modified some of their Steyr-Solothurn guns, received in the early 1930s, by the addition of an under-muzzle bayonet bar. The Type 100's blade was only 200mm(7.87in) long and the

174 Scabbard, 30th year type
175 Sword bayonet, 30th year type, made by Tokyo Arsenal
176 Sword bayonet, 35th year (naval) type, made by Tokyo arsenal c.1903
177 Sword bayonet, 30th year type, by Atsuta subplant of Nagoya arsenal, c.1940
178 Sword bayonet, 30th year type, by Moji subplant of Kokura arsenal; degenerate pattern
179 Scabbard, 30th year type (degenerate)
180 Sword bayonet, 30th year type, degenerate pattern by second Toyoko artillery arsenal
181 Siamese 51st year type bayonet, by Tokyo arsenal, c.1908/10
182 Scabbard, 51st year type

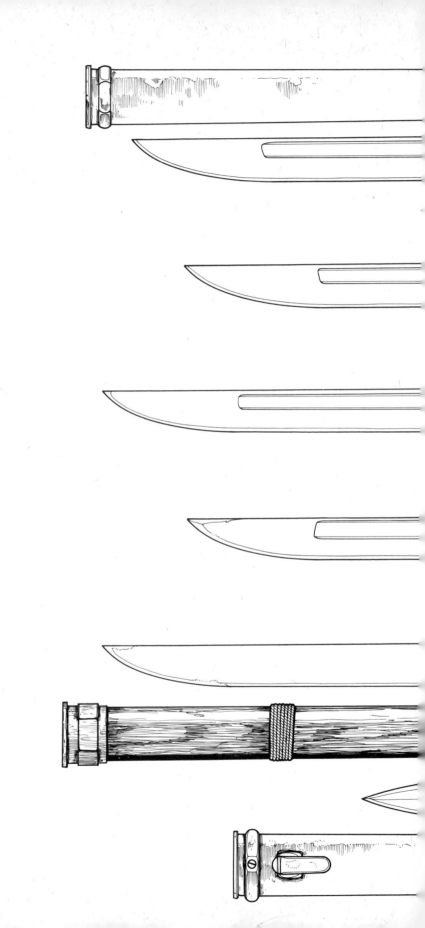

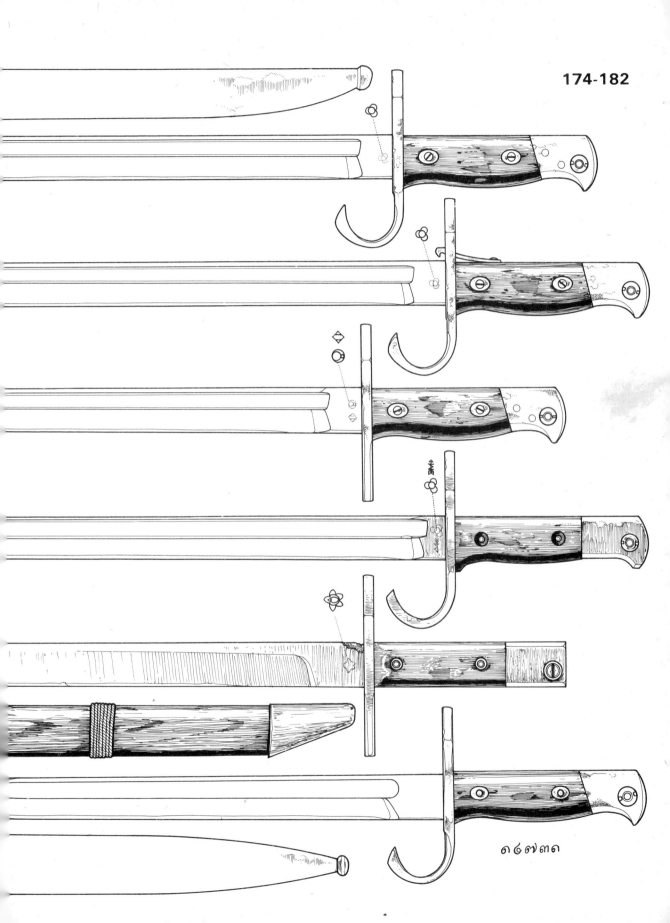

174-182

๑๗๓๓๗

quillon was eliminated from the crossguard; the diameter of the muzzle ring was 14mm(0.551in) and the scabbard was a newly-manufactured short version

Japanese bayonets are usually marked on the ricasso with the device of the manufacturing arsenal, and a list of the more common ones is given later: there is no guarantee that all made bayonets, and insufficient Japanese bayonets have been examined to provide conclusive evidence. A serial number, generally consisting of a Japanese character and five arabic numerals, is often stamped across the end of the pommel.

Copies of the 30th year bayonet were made in North Korea in the period 1950-2. These are quickly recognisable by their manufacture—very similar to the standard quilloned Japanese design but heavier and more clumsy, of inferior material and retaining the grips with ordinary wood screws.

The Netherlands

37. Sword and knife bayonets, 1895

In 1895 the army of the Netherlands adopted a Mannlicher rifle to replace the old Beaumont-Vitali guns then in service. A series of carbines was also adopted, together with an odd variety of bayonets. These, with the exception of the folding bayonet used on the gendarmerie carbines (the 6.5mm Karabijn M1895 aantal 2 OM and NM—M1895 No 2 carbines, old and new models), were sword and knife types and shared two patterns of locking mechanism.

Both seem to draw inspiration from the Rigby-patent design used on the British P1888 sword bayonet, in which an undercut attachment groove is used and in which the mass of the pommel fits between the barrel's undersurface and the bar. The infantry, marines and second-pattern cavalry bayonet all make use of a conventional press-stud mechanism, the stud of which protrudes from the left or reverse side of the pommel.

The second type of locking system makes use of a vertically-moving stud, the head of which appears beneath the bayonets' pommel.

Bajonet M1895, infantry pattern. This has a tapering T-section blade similar in design to that of the French Mle 74 (Gras) épée bayonet, and of a style also used by Greece, Belgium and Denmark. The plain wood grips are held by two large rivets and the first design of guard incorporates a stacking hook (which looks much like a quillon although it was not primarily intended as such); the hooks, however, were abandoned after World War 1 and bayonets of later production were made without them. It is also possible to find some older bayonets from which the stacking hooks have been removed. All M1895 infantry bayonets used pommels of the first type, with the conventional press-stud.

Bajonet M1895, marines' version. The marines' bayonets share the hilt design of the infantry type and make use of the same 360mm (14.13in) blade and 14.5mm(0.571in) muzzle ring. The grips, however, are secured by a single screw which passes through two large oval plates—some 30mm(1.18in) long—to make their removal as easy as possible.

Bajonet M1895, engineers', artillery and cyclists' pattern. This weapon makes use of the second type of locking mechanism in which the stud protrudes from under the pommel. The blade is also longer than the standard, some 480mm(18.90in) compared to 360mm(14.13in), owing to the fact that the bayonet fits a carbine rather than a rifle. The bayonets' overall length is 603mm(23.74in).

Bajonet M1895, cavalry. The knife bayonets issued to the cavalry exist in two forms: those of early manufacture use the pommels of the long M1895 bayonet, with the press-stud under the pommel, while later weapons use the more conventional mechanism found on the M1895 infantry bayonets. Some bayonets

183 Bajonet M1895, infantry pattern
184 Scabbard M95, infantry type
185 Bajonet M95, marines' pattern
186 Bajonet M95, cavalry, with first-type hilt
187 Bajonet M95, engineers', artillery and cyclists' type: made by the governments arsenal at Hembrug

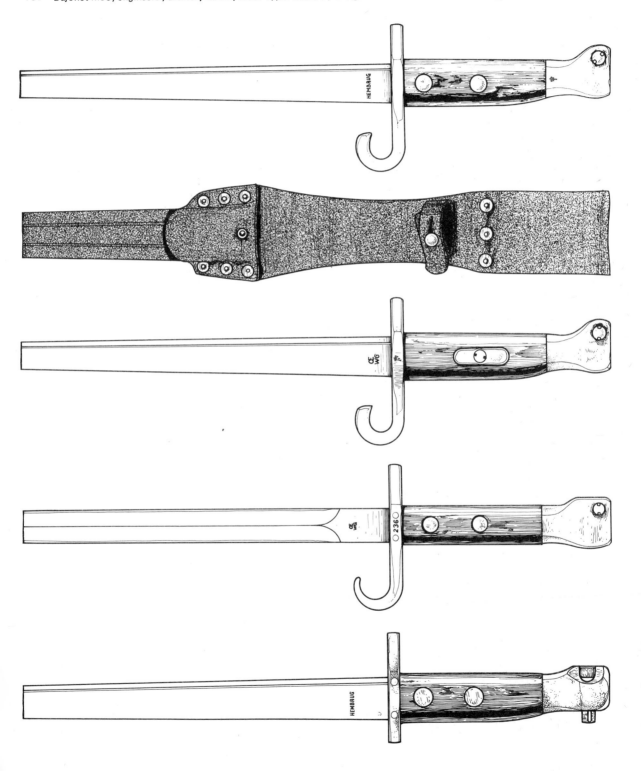

were also given stacking hooks attached to the guard, although this practice was discontinued after World War 1 and the hooks were removed from some of the earlier pieces. Most cavalry bayonets utilise wood grips, retained by two steel washers, but between the wars some were made with composition grips. All, however, have 240mm (9.45in) blades.

Most Dutch bayonets were made by the royal arsenal at Hembrug and as a result they bear the word *Hembrug* on the reverse ricasso. Some were produced prior to 1914 by Österreichische Waffenfabrik Gesellschaft of Steyr (marked OE over WG), while a much smaller number were made in Solingen by Alexander Coppel & Cie; these are marked with Coppel's trademark of balanced scales.

Scabbards for all these bayonets are of plain russet leather with integral belt frogs riveted to the scabbard body, and end in small steel ferrules. Copper-wire binding usually appears for a short distance above the ferrule, and most of the scabbards have retaining loops to hold the bayonets' hilt.

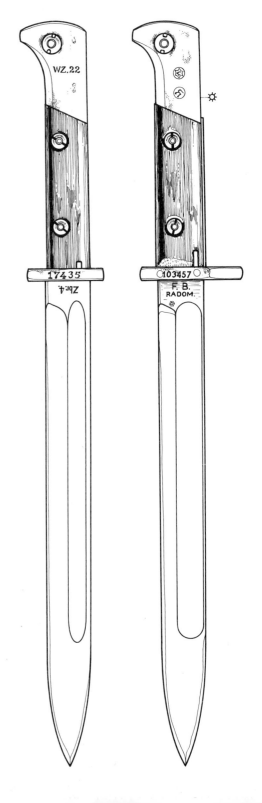

188 Bayonet wz/22, number 17435, made by 'Zbr.' 4'
189 Bayonet wz/29, made at Radom, number 103457. The right side of the pommel and the face of the scabbard bear Israeli marks

Poland

38. Knife bayonets, 1922–1945

The Russian October Revolution, combined with the result of World War 1, conspired to give Poland independence. The Polish army was at first armed with quantities of Russian Mosin-Nagant and German Mauser rifles, some of which were captured, others donated as war reparation, and still others which had been in the ex-Russian arsenals by then in Poland; the Poles also received the rifle-making machinery from the Germans' former Königlich Gewehrfabrik (royal arsenal) at Danzig, which was installed in a new factory at Radom. The first rifles to be produced at Radom were copies of the German Gew 98 and Kar 98, and were apparently called wz/22 or wz/98/22 by the Polish army (wz being the abbreviation for wzor, or 'model'). Many of the ex-Russian Mosin-Nagant rifles were shortened, altered, and fitted with Mauser-type bayonet bands under the title wz/25 (the designation wz/91/98/25—perhaps a manufacturing pattern, or merely a Western fabrication—is also often used for these guns). The old-pattern Mauser rifles were produced until 1929, when the Poles copied the Czech vz/24 rifle as the Karabin wz/29.

Several different patterns of bayonet exist, all of essentially similar design, but a lack of known designations makes it very difficult to provide categoric statements of which preceded which. The presence on the pommels of various stamps—for example WZ 22, WZ 24, WZ 27 or WZ 29—makes the matter still worse. It is thought that the designation **wz/22** represents the original type, which apparently existed in two distinct models: one, with a flashguard but without a muzzle ring, intended specifically for the 1922 Polish model of the German Kar 98 (whose bayonet hilt protruded past the muzzle) and the other, with a 15.5mm(0.610in) ring but without the guard, was intended for the wz/22 Mauser rifle and for the wz/25 conversion of the Russian o1891g. Bayonets found with both the guard and the muzzle ring are thought to be of the universal **wz/29** pattern intended to fit all the rifles then in service. It is also likely that the Germans removed the muzzle rings from many bayonets, and cases where it is difficult to recognise a very skilful alteration can lead to confusion amongst the designations. A lot also depends on whether the Poles marked their bayonets with model dates based on the year of production (rather than the year of adoption) which could conceivably lead to instances where identical bayonets are stamped WZ 24 and WZ 27, having been manufactured three years apart. Other ordnance departments, Sweden's for example, are known to have done this at various times.

All the bayonets have single-edged fullered blades some 250mm(9.84in) long and plain wood grips held to the steel hilt by two bolts; Mauser-style attachment grooves and internal coil-spring press-studs are used. Though very similar to contemporary German bayonets, the Polish types' grips meet the pommel diagonally. All the metal parts were originally bright-finished and the steel scabbards were painted khaki.

The blades are stamped with the marks of the two manufacturers, Fabryka Bronie w Radomiu—the Radom arms factory, marked F.B. Radom—and a private firm in Warsaw called Perkun, whose marks were Perkun or more rarely Perkun Warszawa. The Polish property stamp W.P., the eagle of Poland, and a five-figure serial number are also generally present. Some weapons have also been noted bearing the stamp Zbr.4, but the significance of this is not known: it may, perhaps, be a form of manufacturers' coding. The mark is known on weapons bearing 'date stamps' as early as 1922. The crossguards of some of the weapons vary in thickness between 5.8mm and 8.1mm(0.228-0.319in), but this does not seem to represent a difference in production between the two manufacturers: both apparently produced bayonets with different guard thicknesses.

During World War 2 many Polish bayonets and rifles were seized by the Wehrmacht; the Polish bayonets, in fact, would fit the German rifles as well as those of Poland, and were generally issued by the Germans with the blade and the hilt heavily blued. The muzzle rings of many were removed in keeping with standard German practice, but it is not known with certainty whether or not their production was continued in a ringless form under German control.

Switzerland

39. Knife bayonets, 1889–1931

The obsolete Swiss Ordonnanz 1889 bayonets, beautifully-made of first-class materials, were issued with the Schmidt-Rubin straight-pull rifles. The bayonet design was most successful: the US Army—having tested designs from Britain, Denmark, Austria-Hungary, Belgium and Japan—adopted the Swiss pattern in 1892 for their Krag-Jørgensen rifle.

There are four variations of the Ordonnanz 1889 differing only in the design of the blade, in that three of the four have various stops in the fullers to engage the blade retaining spring attached within the scabbards' mouthpiece. This difference apart, all the bayonets have 298mm(11.73in) blades and overall lengths of 420mm(16.54in). The blades are single-edged with deep broad fullers and equipped with false edges at the spear points. The hilts, like the blades, have the steel mirror-polished (though individual soldiers were permitted to have the metal parts of their sidearms nickel-plated). The design of the Ordonnanz 1889 is conventional, with a straight crossguard and a muzzle ring 15mm(0.59in) in diameter, plain wooden grips secured by two steel rivets, and a pommel with a pronounced beak. An internal coil-spring press-stud is positioned on the reverse(left) side.

The four bayonets' designations are subject to debate, owing to the appearance in print of several different and contradictory lists. The following represents a summary of the available information, together with notes on the other designations that are known to have been used by some.

Ordonnanz 1889; all agree that this is the original type, without obstruction to the plain fullers, introduced on 26th June 1889.

Ordonnanz 1889/99; this has a spot-welded protrusion in the obverse (right) fuller, added to original 1889 bayonets. A second pattern of this bayonet also exists, sometimes known as the 'Ordonnanz 1899'. In this a rivet was placed through the blade, with the head protruding in the obverse fuller some 25mm(1in) from the hilt end. This weapon is sometimes called 'Model 1896', or 'Model 96/11' after two of the rifles with which it was issued.

Ordonnanz 1911; this pattern has a transverse ridge replacing the rivet or the spot-weld, and was introduced on 13th January 1913. The type is sometimes called the Ordonnanz 1899, but it seems unlikely that the weapon was made so early; it was apparently introduced as an accessory for the Infanterie Gewehr (IG) (*Ordonnanz 19*) 11.

Another bayonet, officially known as the **Ordonnanz 1918,** was introduced at a later date, although it is not known with certainty whether this bayonet was produced in quantity before 1920. The weapon was originally introduced to fit the Karabiner Ordonnanz 1911 (which had initially used the Ordonannz 1914 saw-backed bayonet) and was later used for the Karabiner Ordonnanz 1931. The hilt of the 1918 pattern was similar to that of the 1889 bayonet, but was longer at 131mm(5.16in) and the crossguard had a muzzle ring with a diameter of 14mm(0.55in). The blade was also slightly longer than that of its predecessor (300mm/11.81in) and was of completely different design, having a rhombic or double-edged form similar to those of the British P88 and P03. A few Ordonnanz 1918 bayonets were made by utilising unused hilts from the Ordonnanz 1914 engineers' bayonets; these, although to some extent machined-down, are still broader. The comparative dimension is taken across the grip where the grips meet the pommel: 26mm(1.02in) for the

190   Ordonnanz 89 bayonet, made by Maschinenfabrik Bern, number 195360
191   Obverse guard and ricasso
192   Ordonnanz 89/99 bayonet, with rivet, by SIG of Neuhausen, number 259932
193   Obverse guard and ricasso
194   Ordonnanz 89 scabbard
195   Ordonnanz 11 bayonet, by Waffenfabrik Neuhausen, number 451852
196   Ordonnanz 18 bayonet, by Waffenfabrik Neuhausen, number 782578
197   Obverse guard and ricasso

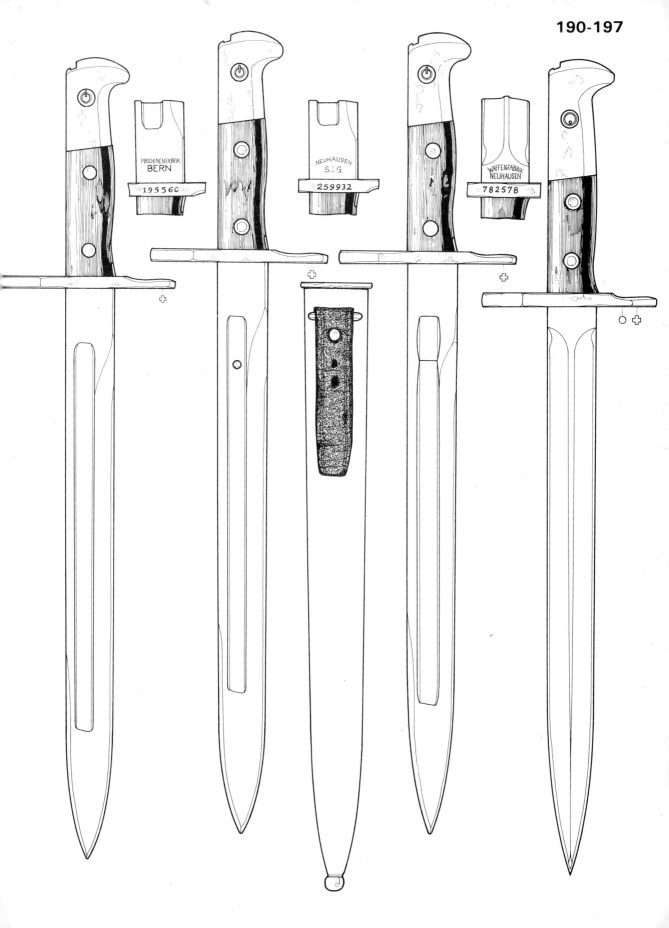

MASCHINENFABRIK
BERN

195360

NEUHAUSEN
S.I.G.

259932

WAFFENFABRIK
NEUHAUSEN

782578

normal pattern but 29mm(1.14in) on the altered type.

The scabbard is the same as that of the Ordonnanz 1889; an all-steel pattern with a leather strap, attached to the scabbard by means of a loop that mated with a buckle on a leather frog. The majority of the bayonets seem to have been made by Schweizerische Industrie-Gesellschaft of Neuhausen-am-Rheinfalls (marked *Waffenfabrik Neuhausen* or *SIG Neuhausen*) and Eidgenössische Waffenfabrik Bern (marked *Waffenfabrik Bern*). Several other markings are known, however, including *Schwarzwaffen Bern* and *Elsener Schweiz Victoria*.

40. Engineers' bayonets, 1906–1914

The two engineers' bayonets are very similar in design, the Modell 1914 evolving from the much rarer Modell 1906. Both are normally referred to by the designation of the Schmidt-Rubin rifles of 1889 and 1911 though both were introduced after the adoption of the actual firearm. The correct designations were the **Säbelbajonett Ordonnanz 1906 für Schmidt-Rubin Gewehre**, designed for the Schmidt-Rubin rifle of 1889 and the **Säbelbajonett Ordonnanz 1914 für Schmidt-Rubin Gewehre** issued with the Schmidt-Rubin of 1911.

The 1906 pattern combined a hilt similar to that of the 1889 infantry bayonet with the blade of the earlier Vetterli engineer bayonets of 1878 and 1887. The hilt, 130mm(5.19in) long, follows the design of the 1889 type and has a 15mm(0.59in) muzzle ring. The saw-backed blade is unusual in that it has only one fuller on the right (or obverse) side; the left, or reverse, remains completely flat. The long fuller runs to within 85mm(3.35in) of the point. The back has a saw of 25 double teeth for 262mm(10.31in) and a false edge from the end of the saw to the point. The blade length is 475mm(18.70in) giving the bayonet an overall length of 605mm(23.82in). It weighs 595gm(21oz), and though heavy when attached to the gun it made an excellent shortsword and tool for the engineers. The issue scabbard is of leather with steel mounts; the top mount has a leather strap, attached to a loop, which engages the buckle of the leather frog.

In 1914 an improved Ordonnanz 1906 bayonet was adopted, designated Ordonnanz 1914. The hilt and blade lengths remained the same but the bayonet weighed considerably more—765gm(27oz). The hilt, while unaltered in length, was broader and stronger, and the muzzle ring for the Schmidt-Rubin carbine of 1911 was 14mm(0.55in) in diameter. The blade retains the single fuller on the obverse (right) side but the fuller is shorter and the point swells into a slight spear shape. The saw-back is longer, with 32 double teeth in a length of 330mm(12.99in). This bayonet also has a steel mounted leather scabbard but the majority were issued with an all-steel scabbard.

The metal surfaces of both bayonets were polished bright but individual soldiers could have their sidearms privately plated if they wished. The serial numbers were stamped on the crossguards; the Swiss cross (Croix de Génève or Geneva Cross) was placed on the crossguards' underside and on the scabbard ferrule, while the manufacturer's name was marked on the right blade ricasso. Most were made at Waffenfabrik Neuhausen.

Turkey

41. Sword bayonet, 1887

German influence and interest in the Balkans and Turkey grew out of the necessity to preserve the balance of power against the ever-present threat of Russia. Turkey was as a result largely armed with weapons of German origin, and indeed much of the army's training was supervised by German specialists. In 1886 the Turkish government contacted Waffenfabrik Mauser AG to arrange the supply of a rifle

198 Ordonnanz 06 engineer's bayonet, number 112038; uses an old Ordonnanz 78 blade
199 Ordonnanz 06 scabbard (old Ordonnanz 84)
200 Ordonnanz 14 engineer's bayonet, by Waffenfabrik Neuhausen
201 Ordonnanz 14 scabbard
202 Bayonet M1887, by Alexander Coppel & Cie, Solingen
203 Bayonet M1890, by Alexander Coppel & Cie, Solingen
204 Scabbard M1887 and M1890
205 Bayonet M1903 (long pattern), by Weyersberg, Kirschbaum & Cie of Solingen
206 Scabbard M1903 (long pattern)
207 Bayonet M1903 (short pattern)
208 Bayonet M1903, all-steel or 'Ersatz' type, c.1915/16
209 Scabbard M1903 (short)

comparable to the Infanteriegewehr Modell 71/84 then in the hands of the German army, and the result was the Turkish rifle M1887 which fired a 9.5mm blackpowder cartridge and used an under-barrel tube magazine. The Turks ordered no fewer than 500000 rifles and 50000 carbines, the contract being spilt between Waffenfabrik Mauser and Ludwig Loewe & Cie, but the introduction in Germany of the Gew 88 made the Turks implement a protection clause in the contract—guarding against the introduction in Germany of an improved weapon—and the order for the M1887 was cancelled in 1890 after some 220000 rifles and carbines had been delivered. The 7.65mm M1890 rifle was purchased instead. Mauser and Loewe thereafter finished the Turkish rifles that were in course of production when the cancellation was received, and the weapons were placed in store (it is thought that about 25000 were completed after 1890). In World War 1 the surviving rifles, together with their Turkish bayonets, were taken from store and issued to the Landsturm of Württemberg. These are usually stamped *Deutschland* or *Deutsch* in addition to their original Turkish marks. A symbolised deer's antler, part of Württemberg's coat-of-arms, was also sometimes used.

The M1887 Turkish bayonet is conventional in design, with a single-edged blade some 464mm (18.25in) long; the blade, which tapered slightly towards the point, was fullered on both sides. The bayonet's overall length was about 597mm (23.50in). The hilt is of steel and has plain wood grips held by two steel rivets set in washers. The pommel has a T-slot and a standard internal coil-spring press-stud protruding from the obverse or right side, while the crossguard's sweptforward quillon ends in a ball finial. The diameter of the muzzle ring is 16.5mm (0.650in) and the distance between the top of the ring and the back of the hilt—27mm (1.063in)—provides the principal means of distinguishing the M1887 from the later M1890.

The scabbard is of black leather with steel mounts, and has an overall length of 476mm (18.75in). The mounts are stapled to the body, and each possesses four decorative lines scribed around it. The scabbard has an oval frog-stud and the blade retaining spring,

contained within the topmount, is held by a single screw on the mount's face.

The bayonet cannot be mistaken for anything other than Turkish from its markings: the star and crescent motif appears on the pommel, together with the *Toughra,* while on the reverse ricasso appears the name of the manufacturer and the date of production, both in arabic script. Translation of the markings usually indicate either Weyersberg, Kirschbaum & Cie or Alexander Coppel & Cie (both of Solingen) although a third—as yet unidentified—type has been seen.

42. Sword bayonets, 1890–1903

Following improvements to the Mauser rifle, Turkey took delivery of its new 7.65mm model 1890 Mauser only three years after adopting the original 9.5mm pattern. The model 1890 bayonet was issued with the new rifle, but remained very similar to the previous type of 1887. The 1890 bayonet would, in fact, also fit the rifles of 1893 (a variation of the Spanish gun of the same year), 1903 and 1905.

The model 1890 bayonet is identical to the 1887 type with the exceptions of the crossguard and the muzzle ring. The overall length of the bayonet is 590mm(23.23in) with a blade measuring 463mm (18.23in). It has a steel hilt with wooden grips, and the crossguard has a swept-forward quillon. The muzzle ring is 16mm(0.63in) in diameter and is further from the back of the hilt than that of the model 1887; the muzzle ring is, in fact, about 38mm(1.50in) from the back of the 1890 hilt. The steel-mounted leather scabbard, 475mm(18.70in) long, is identical to that of the earlier weapon.

In 1890 a 'bayonet' was also issued to the musicians of the Turkish army, although (since it could not be fitted to any of the service rifles) this was no more than a dress sidearm. It is identical to the infantry model, but it has neither a press-stud nor a bar attachment groove and the muzzle ring—which has a diameter of 14.5mm(0.57in)—serves no purpose other than to give the appearance of a bayonet. In all

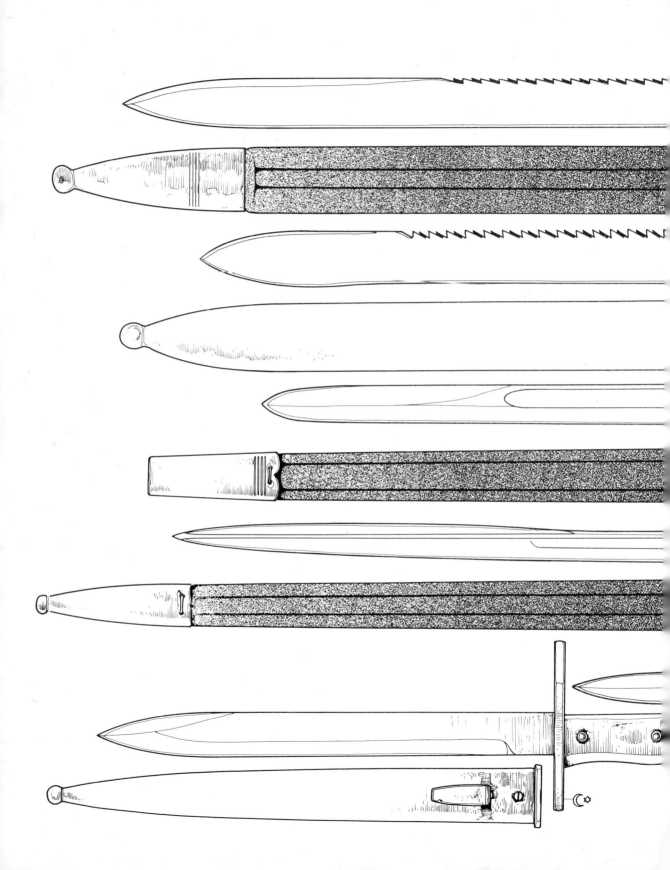

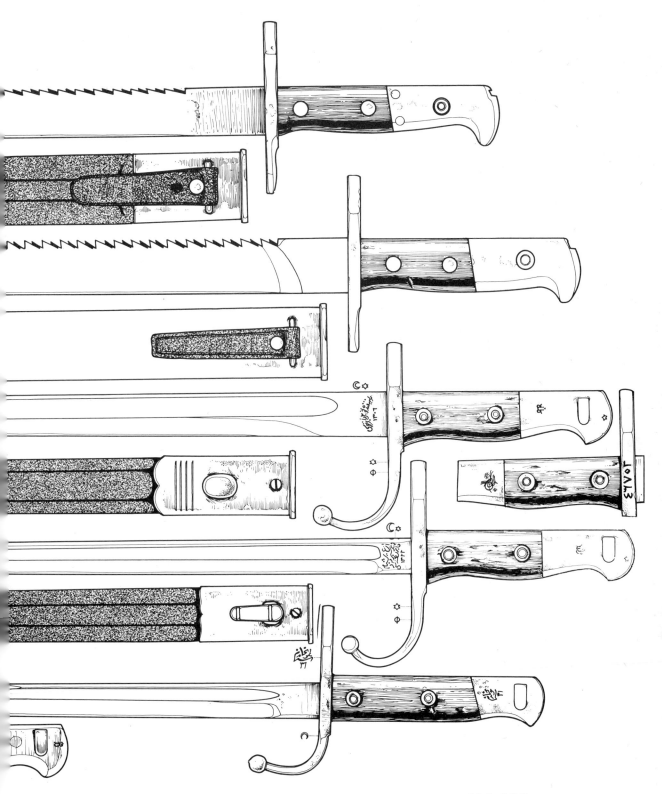

198-209

other respects, however, the 1890 musicians' sidearm is the model 1890 bayonet.

Thirteen years later the long model 1903 bayonet was adopted by the Turks together with a new rifle, very similar to the Germans' G98. The bayonet blade was also patterned after the German original, but the hilt of the weapon was that used with the Turkish 1890 bayonets. The blade is 525mm (20.67in) long and exceptionally slim, being no more than 18mm (0.71in) wide for some 305mm (12.00in) of its length, with a single edge, a fuller on each side and a pipe-back; the last 220mm (8.66in) of the blade swells to a point comparable to that of the British Lancaster Sappers' and Miners' Carbine pattern of 1855, but it is much slimmer. The spear point's maximum width is also 18mm (0.71in) as the true edge slopes upwards at the point and finishes level with the pipeback.

The scabbard is of black leather with steel mounts similar to those of the German original. The topmount, however, measures 62.5mm (2.44in) compared to the 50.6mm (1.99in) of the German S98. The overall length of the scabbard is 545mm (21.46in) while that of the bayonet is 652mm (25.67in).

Both the 1890 and the 1903 pattern bayonets can be found with the blades shortened and repointed; no official order has been found sanctioning these but it is possible that such did occur during World War 1, especially when the Germans began to supply the short Ersatz weapons.

The markings on the bayonets are similar to those on the model 1887. A star and a crescent are usually found on the pommel and elsewhere, while a unique device known as the *Toughra* (basically the ruler's cypher) appears on the pommel's obverse (or right) side. The name of the manufacturers, together with the date of manufacture, are to be found in arabic script on the ricasso. The bayonets were exclusively produced in Germany and translations of the blade inscriptions usually read either Weyersberg, Kirschbaum & Cie or Alexander Coppel & Cie (both of Solingen).

Many Turkish bayonets are now found without their scabbards: possibly they were snatched as souvenirs from bodies or prisoners, where there was not enough time to detach the scabbards from the belts. This, conceivably, could have been the case in places such as Gallipoli.

43. Knife bayonets, 1903–1918

The Turkish M1903 short bayonet is often described as a conversion of the long M1903, but (although shortened and repointed M1887, M1890 and M1903

bayonets are often found) the true short M1903 was newly manufactured with a blade of 250mm (9.85in). The blade is single-edged, with a double-edged point, and has a crudely-cut fuller on each side.

The hilt, including the crossguard, is 125mm (4.87in) long and has a steel guard with a slender sweptforward quillon that ends in a small ball finial. The plain wood grips are held in place by two steel rivets set into domed washers; they meet the pommel diagonally. The pommel has a T-groove and an internal coil-spring press-stud that protrudes from the obverse or right side. The overall length of the weapon is 376mm (14.80in).

The steel scabbard measures 273mm (10.75in) and tapers, to end in a round brass ferrule. The frog-stud is also of brass and the blade retaining springs are held in the scabbard by a single screw, on the scabbard face above the stud. There are no markings on the scabbard or the bayonet, with the exception of the star and crescent motif which appears on the cross-guard.

During World War 1 an all-steel Ersatz bayonet was produced and supplied by the Germans to the Turks. This bayonet has a 250mm (9.85in) fullerless blade and is sharpened to a double-edge point. The hilt is 123mm (4.81in) long and is made entirely of steel. The crossguard is straight, and has a muzzle ring with a diameter of 15.5mm (0.610in). The hilt is attached to the blade tang by two large steel rivets and has both a standard internal coil-spring press-stud and a T-groove.

The all-steel scabbard is 273mm (10.75in) long and has a small ridge around its edge together with a small ferrule at its tip. There is no mouthpiece but the retaining springs are themselves retained by a single screw above the frog-stud. The scabbard and hilt of these bayonets are usually found painted either field-grey or brown; there is generally a German inspection marking on the obverse or right side of the blade and a star-and-crescent on the cross-guard.

Turkey, like Germany, was also in need during the war of extra supplies, and consequently Germany passed many of her obsolete rifles to the Turks. Thus many old German bayonets—such things, for example as the brass-hilted Modell 1871—can be found with Turkish marks in addition to their old German ones.

Union of Soviet Socialist Republics

44. Sword bayonet, 1936 (AVS)

During the last years of the 1920s and the beginning of the 1930s the Russians undertook extensive experiments with the intention of designing suitable self-loading rifles that could then be issued to the Red Army. The outcome of the trials suggested that two of the competing designs, the Simonov and the Tokarev, were worthy of further trials. Small numbers of each were made in 1931 and 1932 respectively and issued to the forces, and in 1936 manufacture of the Simonov-designed AVS o1936g (the Avtomaticheskaia Vintovka Simonova, or Simonov automatic rifle, M1936) was commenced. It is thought that about 10000 AVS rifles were made in the period 1936-8 before the Russians decided that the design was not a success. The guns were then discarded, although survivors were used in the Russo-Finnish 'Winter War' of 1939-40 and in the opening stages of the Great Patriotic War (1941-5). None were ever used outside Russia.

The AVS's bayonet, called the *shtik o1936g*, has a double-edged knife blade with a length of 332mm (13.06in), giving the bayonet an overall length of 465mm (18.30in). The fullers, somewhat unusually, are placed diagonally and taper slightly towards the point. Close to the hilt is a rectangular forged depression in which is placed the bayonet's serial number.

The steel hilt has wooden grips held in place by a single slotted-head bolt; the central portion is finely chequered to improve the handgrip. The attachment mechanism is most unusual, indeed unique; a hook at the end of the pommel fits over a round bar positioned beneath the barrel at a right angle to its length. A spring-loaded lever at the pommel clips the bar through the hook so that the bayonet hangs pivoted from the bar. The bayonet is swung forward until a second hook placed at the muzzle clips into a rectangular opening cut into the back of the bayonet. This holds the bayonet securely, but is a very complicated way of achieving it.

The scabbard for the o1936g is made completely of steel and follows the contours of the blade, although it swells slightly at the mouthpiece to protect the hilt of the bayonet.

The AVS bayonet was an extremely complicated pattern, mirroring the design of the rifle with which it was issued: the Russians generally favoured simplicity, and so both the Simonov rifle and its peculiar bayonet were abandoned in favour of the Tokarev-type SVT.

45. Sword and knife bayonets, 1938–1940 (SVT)

The first issue Tokarev rifle was the SVT o1938g (Samozariadniya Vintovka Tokareva, or Tokarev self-loading rifle), introduced to replace the unsuccessful AVS. Three patterns of the Tokarev rifle were produced—the SVT o1938g, the SVT o1940g and the AVT o1940g — and all saw service through the war as NCOs' weapons, from which the design emerged with a reputation for mechanical reliability but a certain weakness of construction. The rifles weighed less than 4.00kg(8.82lb) and were hence very lightly built for their size.

Two types of bayonet, identical in all but blade length, are known to have been issued with the weapons; convention dictates that the longer bayonet should be called the o1938g and the shorter the o1940g, but it seems that the Russians draw a distinction only in the manufacturing pattern. Both types seem to have been called the *shtik o1938g*, and it is apparent that the reduction in blade length occurred as a result of a desire to conserve vital material which was otherwise put to a useless purpose. The change probably occurred in 1941.

Both the long and short-bladed models have single-edged blades ending in double-edged points, one 362mm(14.25in) long and the other only 244mm(9.62in) long. In both types the fullers' top edges are parallel to the blade, but the bottom edges slope upward towards the point and the resulting tapered fullers give the illusion of being slightly diagonal. The small crossguard, held to the tang by two steel rivets (the heads of which are sometimes found ground flush), has a muzzle ring with a diameter of 13.7mm(0.539in). The steel hilt has wood grips held to the tang by two slotted-head bolts. The design and manufacture of the hilt and the press-stud are a little unusual: the construction of the pommel/tang joint, so often achieved either by brazing or by riveting, is accomplished by mating a round vertical 'key' with a similar hole in the pommel (see drawing), and the press-stud is set into a partially-shrouded housing that effectively prevents it being accidentally depressed.

Both types of bayonet have steel scabbards in which the belt frogs were riveted to the backs; most frogs, originally of leather, were made of webbing in wartime.

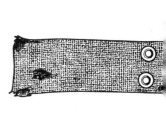

46. Folding bayonet, 1944

The Russians retained their o1891g socket bayonet long after the Western powers had adopted knife and sword types. In 1930 the Soviets had added a spring-loaded locking mechanism in place of the original locking ring, but the basic bayonet remained un-altered through the whole of World War 2. The personnel of the Red Army were not issued with scabbards for their socket bayonets, which were always carried in the fixed position: the rifles' sights, in fact, were corrected to compensate for the effects of the bayonet on the barrel vibrations and hence on the flight of the bullet.

It was only natural, therefore, that a folding bayonet would be designed for one of the Russian firearms—and so one was fitted to the Mosin-Nagant carbine of 1944. The 1944-pattern bayonet has a cruciform blade of 311mm(12.25in), an overall length of 384mm(15.13in), andis of exceptionally simple design. It can be folded or fixed in position by sliding a spring-loaded tube (which incorporates the muzzle ring) away from the pivot block. This disengages the locking projection on the pivot block from the corresponding notch on the sliding tube, and permits the bayonet to be swung forward or back: there are at least two minor variants of the locking mechanism, because weapons are known in which the locking projection is on the tube rather than on the pivot block. The muzzle ring, part of the sliding tube, moves beyond the muzzle as the tube is pushed forward and then springs back to rest against the hooded foresight.

210-217

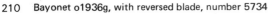

210   Bayonet o1936g, with reversed blade, number 5734
211   Obverse ricasso
212   Scabbard o1936g
213   Bayonet o1938g (long), VD3623
214   Bayonet o1938g (short, c.1942), reversed blade type, L53155
215   Bottom view of the hilt
216   Bayonet o1938g (short, c.1942) with conventional blade, B40327
217   Bayonet o1944g

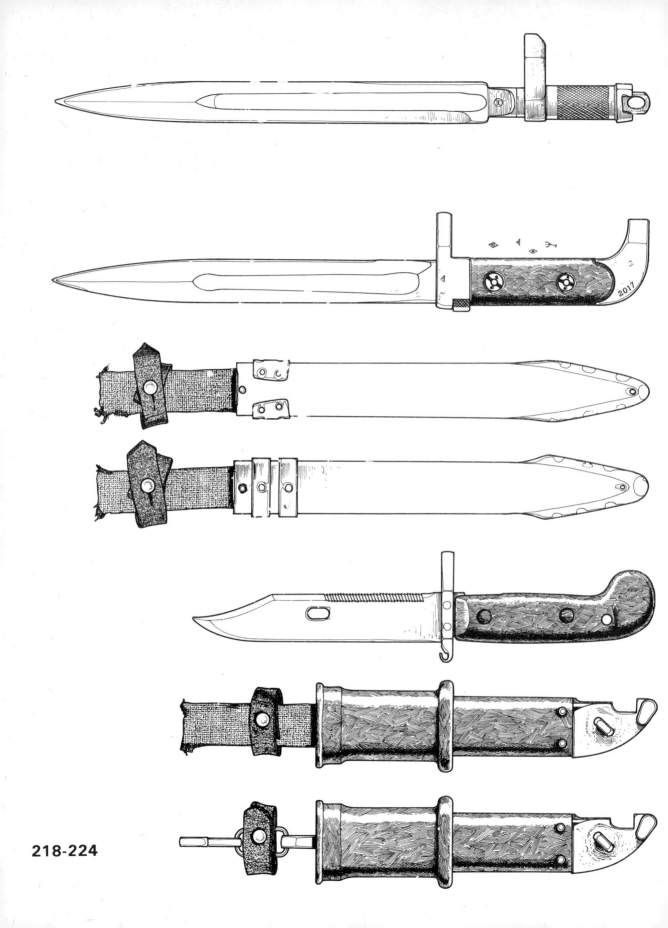

218-224

47. Folding bayonet, 1946–1956 (SKS)

The introduction in wartime Germany of an intermediate cartridge, the Pist Patr 43 , caused the Russians to develop a similar round—introduced as the o1943g (*i.e.* model of 1943), although it did not appear until c.1945. The first weapon to be chambered for the new cartridge was the Simonov semiautomatic carbine, the SKS or Samozariadniya Karabin Simonova, the first supplies of which reached the troops in 1946/7. The SKS, or copies of it, has since been extensively used throughout the Soviet bloc: Bulgaria and the German Democratic Republic have both produced the weapon, in the latter case as the Karabiner Simonow or Kar S, and the Chinese People's Republic has manufactured the weapon as the Type 56 carbine (not to be confused with the Type 56 and Type 56/1 assault rifles, copies of the AK). In addition the Simonov has appeared in Yugoslavia as the M59 and M59/66, in Albania, in Vietnam, in Indonesia and in Cuba.

The bayonet used with all the SKS variations, with the exception of the Chinese Type 56 (a second pattern of folding bayonet) and the Yugoslav M59/66 (none), was a folding pattern based on that of the o1944g Mosin-Nagant carbine: its locking mechanism for attaching and folding the bayonet is virtually identical. The sliding hilt-tube is improved by the addition of fine chequering to the central portion, materially improving the grip, but the bayonet still retains the muzzle ring, the pivot and the internal coil-spring of the o1944g. The blade, some 222mm(8.75in) long, is single-edged for the greater part of its length but has a double-edged point. The whole blade surface is of phosphated steel, which gives it a distinctive matt finish; the two 145mm(5.71in) fullers are placed centrally on the blade, and the muzzle ring has a diameter of 14mm(0.551in). The point, when folded, fits into a groove in the fore-end of the wooden stock.

The Chinese Type 56 carbine bayonet is described separately, but differs from its Russian prototype in that it uses a triangular blade some 305mm(12.00in) long. The Russian-type SKS bayonet was also used on the United Arab Republic's 'Rashid' rifle, which

although based on their 'Hakim' (and therefore a Ljungmann-system gun rather than a Simonov) utilises the Russian o1943g cartridge and various fittings from the SKS—including the bayonet. None of these bayonets were marked.

48. Knife and folding bayonets, 1947–1970 (AK)

The AK full- automatic rifle rapidly superseded the semiautomatic SKS and was issued and made in wide variety of satellite and Soviet-aligned countries: the AK, however, has now itself been replaced by a much lightened derivative, the AKM or Avtomat Kalashnikova Modificatsionnii (modified Kalashnikov assault rifle), which is also produced by some of the bloc countries.

The prototype AK was not designed with a bayonet, but the Soviets then decided that one should be added; the result was a slightly unconventional knife bayonet used by all the various AK and AK-derivative weapons, except those that were not fitted for a bayonet at all and the Chinese Type 56 and 56/1 assault rifles' folding bayonets. The blade, 200mm(7.87in) long, is a typical Soviet design with a blunt point and a phosphated steel finish; the fullers are placed centrally but the cutting edge is uppermost, a practice reminiscent of some Czechoslovak and Austro-Hungarian patterns. The blued steel hilt has plain plastic grips, rounded at the pommel and held in place by two slotted-head bolts similar to those used on British bayonets. There is a muzzle ring, with a diameter of 17.5mm(0.689in), but here all claims to conventionality cease: the pommel sweeps upwards into two 'ears' which, when the bayonet is fixed, slide down the barrel to fit round the cleaning rod and piston housing bracket attached to the barrel. The cleaning rod fits into a groove cut along the back of the bayonet's grips and the muzzle ring then clips over the barrel; two prongs within the open back of the hilt are operated by a catch at the base of the rudimentary crossguard to engage with the foresight base and the cleaning rod block, thus locking the bayonet firmly in position. Both ends of the catch are chequered to facilitate operation, which is easily effected. The metal scabbard is painted black and has a webbing belt frog with a press-fastener and a loop to hold the bayonet in the scabbard. The frog is attached to two metal loops positioned at the back of the scabbard.

Some AK bayonets bear a serial number consisting of a letter and four numbers, but many are unmarked.

The Russians have also introduced a knife bayonet for their SVD sniper's rifle introduced c.1968; the bayonet has a short knife blade, fullered and approximately 130mm (5.19in) long, with a saw-back and an aperture at the tip. This fits over a lug on the tip of the scabbard and then acts as a wire cutter, very similar in concept to the NWM/Eickhorn development for the Stoner automatic rifle: the Russian bayonet probably provided the basis for the Western design. The SVD bayonet has a neo-conventional hilt and a crossguard with a muzzle ring. Few of these bayonets have yet appeared in the west, and rumours that some AKM assault rifles have been modified to take the bayonet are as yet unconfirmed.

Note: Chinese SKS and AK bayonets

The Chinese-made Type 56 carbine, a copy of the Soviets' SKS, originally used an exact copy of the Russian folding bayonet (although of slightly cruder finish than the original). Later guns, however, used a Chinese modification of the basic bayonet in which the original locking mechanism was combined with a new blade. The blade is 305mm(12.00in) long and is again of treated steel, giving it a dull smooth finish; it is made by taking a tapering rod of round section and machining into it three deep concave fullers, resulting in the appearance of a triangular blade. The blade tapers to a chisel point, placed horizontally, which is some 7mm(0.28in) wide. The whole bayonet is well-finished and equal to the original Soviet type; there are no markings on the weapon.

The Chinese also designed and manufactured a folding bayonet for their Type 56 and 56-1 assault rifles (the latter with a folding stock), which were based on the Russian AK and must not be confused with the Chinese Type 56 carbine—which is an altogether different weapon. The triangular blade, of similar form to that of the second-type Chinese Type 56 carbine bayonet, measures only some 222mm(8.74in) and tapers to a 3.5mm(0.14in) wide chisel point: this has a vertical axis opposed to the horizontal pattern found on the Type 56 carbine. The bayonet retains the sliding tube with the pivot-catch,

AK, AKM, AND AK-TYPE ASSAULT RIFLES

country: type and designation: bayonet

Bulgaria: AK, native-built: standard knife type
Chinese People's Republic: Type 56 assault rifle, native-built: standard knife type
Chinese People's Republic: Type 56 assault rifle, native-built: special folding bayonet
Chinese People's Republic: Type 56-1 assault rifle, native built: special folding bayonet or no bayonet
Cuba: AK, Russian-built: standard knife bayonet
Finland: Rynnäkkökivääri M1960, native modification of AK: M1960 knife bayonet
Finland: Rynnäkkökivääri M1962, native modification of AK: M1962 knife bayonet
German Democratic Republic: MPi K, native-built: standard knife bayonet
German Democratic Republic: MPi KM, native-built: standard knife bayonet
Hungary: AKM 63, native-built: standard knife bayonet?
Hungary: AMD, native-built submachine-gun derivative of AKM: no bayonet
North Korea: AK, native-built: standard knife bayonet
Poland PMK, native-built AK: standard knife bayonet
Poland: PMK-DGN, as above with an integral grenade launcher: no bayonet
Poland: PMKM, native-built AKM: standard knife bayonet
Romania: AK, Russian built: standard knife bayonet
Romania: AKM, native-built: standard knife bayonet
UAR (Egypt, Syria): AK, Russian-built: standard knife bayonet
UAR (Egypt, Syria): AKM, Russian-built: standard knife bayonet
USSR: AK: standard knife bayonet
USSR: AKM: standard knife bayonet or SVD pattern (?)
Yugoslavia: M64 assault rifle, native-built: standard knife bayonet
Yugoslavia: M64A submachine-gun, native-built: no bayonet
Yugoslavia: M64B submachine-gun, native-built: no bayonet

but completely discards the muzzle ring; the tube has a raised bracket with a right-angle arm facing backwards, towards the pivot, on either side of which are three small stepped projections to aid grip. As the bayonet is pivoted towards the fixed position, the bracket arm clips over two prongs attached to the base of the foresight band to hold the bayonet firmly in position. Owing to the fact that the two prongs clip under the bracket, a portion of the top of the sliding tube is cut away and grooves are machined into the tang of the bayonet to make room for the prongs. Two opposed grooves are cut into the base of bayonet, possibly to collect débris that could collect and jam the mechanism or perhaps simply to lighten it. Both the native Chinese folding bayonets date from c.1958-60, and have since been widely used on weapons supplied by China to combatants in the Far East: others have appeared in Africa and in the Middle East.

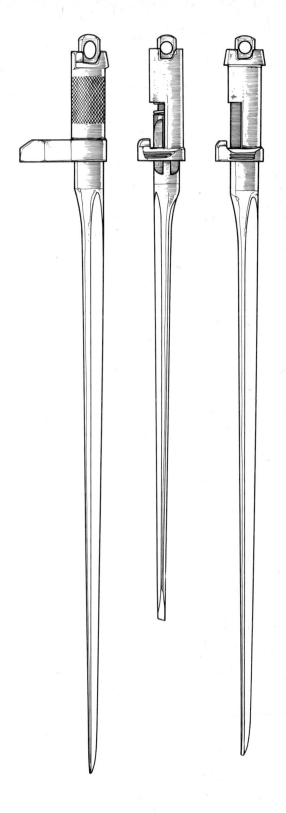

225   Chinese Type 56 (SKS) folding bayonet
226   Chinese Type 56 (AK) folding bayonet
227   Chinese Type 68 folding bayonet: this, the latest Chinese pattern, is used with a rifle that combines features of the AK and the SKS

225-227

United Kingdom

49. Sword bayonet, Pattern 1888

During the summer of 1888 troop trials were carried out with the Lee-Metford rifle and on 22nd December it was officially approved for adoption as the Rifle, Magazine, Mark 1. A knife bayonet was also approved, although it was still designated a sword pattern. Many different designations have appeared in print to describe the various examples of the Sword Bayonet Pattern 1888, and so the classifications used here are taken from the *War Office Tables of Small Arms in use in the British Service, April 1910.*

The first bayonet issued was the **Pattern 1888 Mark 1.** This, like its successors, had a 12in(305mm) double-edged blade strengthened by a medial rib. The short crossguard had a muzzle ring 0.65in(16.5mm) in diameter, stepped back to add strength, and the short quillon had a small finial facing towards the blade. The steel pommel was a departure from conventional design: the bar-attachment groove faced downwards and the back of the pommel was curved to fit close to the rifle barrel. The plain walnut grips were retained by three brass rivets; one large rivet was positioned centrally within 0.5in(12.7mm) of the crossguard while the two small rivets were placed alongside each other at the same distance from the pommel. All Lee-Metford Rifles—whether Marks 1, 1*, 2, 2* or Charger Loading Mark 2—were equipped with cleaning rods , and as the rods protruded beyond the bayonet attachment bars a round hole was cut into the bayonets' hilt. The oiling and cleaning hole was consequently placed through the grips at the end of the groove.

The second bayonet issued was still designated the **Pattern 1888 Mark 1,** but the grips were improved by the introduction of two rivets that replaced the three on the earlier example. The large rivet remained unaltered but the two smaller ones were replaced by a second large one, positioned just below the oil hole in the grips.

Meanwhile modifications were made to the rifles which directly affected the design of the bayonet. April 1890 saw the introduction of a pullthrough for cleaning the barrel and on 22nd February 1892 the cleaning rod was reclassified as a clearing rod (for removing jammed fired cartridge cases), for at the end

of January 1892 the Mark 2 Lee-Metford rifle had been approved—being manufactured with a completely new and shorter rod designed solely for clearing the barrel. Cordite eventually replaced black powder and a new barrel with a different form of rifling was developed at Enfield to suit the altered ballistics of the new cartridges. This rifle, with its new barrel, was introduced on 11th November 1895 as the Rifle Magazine, Lee-Enfield Mark 1, and continued to use either of the P1888 Mark 1 bayonets. On 19th May 1899 the Mark 1* Lee-Enfield was introduced, without a clearing rod.

The alteration to the rifle meant that the long hole in the hilt of the Mk 1 bayonets was no longer necessary, as the pommel's groove had only to fit over the bayonet bar. The **P88 Mk 2** bayonet was consequently introduced, identical to the Mk 1 except that the cleaning hole was placed through the pommel and the two brass rivets holding the grips were placed further apart.

The last modification to the bayonet was made with the introduction of the **P88 Mk 3**. The earlier bayonets had all their metal parts bright-finished but the Mk 3 had the hilt, the crossguard and the first 0.25in(6mm) of the blade blued or browned. The brass rivets of the Mk 2, to facilitate reblueing, were replaced by two steel bolts. The Mk 3, like the Mk 2, had the hole through the pommel. A few Mk 3 bayonets exist with the hole through the grips (in similar fashion to the Mk 1) but these are not bayonets adopted by the British service prior to World War 1. Some Mk 1 specimens were later altered, to bring them up to date, but these were modified for the commercial market. Stocks of thus altered bayonets were found in the 1950s at the firm of W W Greener of Birmingham.

Four different scabbards were approved for issue with the various Pattern 1888 bayonets. The one most widely issued, and also often seen in service with the Pattern 1903, was the **Scabbard P88 (Mk 1) L**. The 'L' denoted 'Land' usage as opposed to the naval scabbard. The land pattern had a brown or black leather body gathered into a pronounced seam and stitched at the back. A steel chape was attached to the body by two staples and a topmount, similarly attached, had an oval frog-stud and contained two blade retaining springs. At the same time a **Scabbard**

P.88 Naval (Mk 1) was adopted for those bayonets issued to naval personnel. This differed from the land pattern in two respects; the frog stud had its surface finely chequered and the tip of the scabbard was completely redesigned, to prevent moisture gathering in the steel mount. Instead the stitching continued almost to the tip where it enclosed a leather plug that was also additionally secured by a brass pin passing through the end of the scabbard body. Two more land pattern scabbards were adopted but both were issued only in very limited quantities. The **Scabbard P88 Land (Mk 2)** used the same brown leather body as the naval Mark 1 but the steel topmount had no frog-stud; the whole mount was instead enclosed within a leather band tightly sewn on and attached by a single staple. A shaped flap formed part of the band at the back, with an eyelet and a brass stud that enabled it to be attached to the belt. The **Scabbard P88 Land (Mk 2*)** was similar in all respects, except that attached to a narower flap by two brass rivets was a leather belt-loop. This loop had two eyelets, one completely through it and one only at its back, which helped to hold the bayonet securely in position on the belt.

By 1904 some of the Pattern 1888 bayonets still in service were issued with Pattern 1903 scabbards described later. The 1904 *Text Book of Small Arms* describes the P88 Mk 3 bayonet as being issued with **Scabbard P03 Land (Mk 1)**.

Many variations of the P.1888 bayonets were manufactured solely for the commercial market and these should not be confused with the bayonets previously described: the only ones issued to British forces. In the past these have been erroneously described as of Indian manufacture—but they are British-made in most cases for the large commercial trade in arms at the turn of the century. They are often of poor quality and are usually devoid of markings. Muzzle ring diameters vary considerably, as does the length of the blades. A few are marked *Ontex* on the blades, the tradename of an unknown maker; W W Greener of Birmingham bought large stocks of surplus or unfinished P88, bayonets as well as large stocks of the parts. These were assembled at their works and sold commercially, being usually stamped *W W Greener Birmingham* on the blade and on the back of the hilt between the grips; the pommels were often stamped *Pat '88*. As these weapons were made up from genuine parts it is not uncommon to find the blades stamped with the original maker's name as well as Greener's trademark.

Old British inspection marks may be present and in a few cases the marriage of parts has produced a hilt with two cleaning holes—one through the grips and another through the pommel. These bayonets are well finished and their scabbards have removable mouthpieces held in place by a screw through the topmount. Occasionally a retailer's name appears either on the blade or on the grips. Apart from the Greener bayonets (which are easily identified) the poor quality of the majority of commercial bayonets based on the P88 design and the lack of British markings prevent any confusion with the original service bayonets.

50. Sword bayonet, Pattern 1903

The British Army, anxious to improve upon their long Lee-Enfield rifles, studied a report of June 1900 on the weapon's drawbacks submitted by the Small Arms Committee. The result was the approval, on 12th January 1901, of the manufacture of 1000 'shortened Modified Enfield Rifles'; the army ultimately adopted the rifle, as standard issue, on 23rd December 1902 but further problems of accuracy led to the cancellation of the initial design and the approval on 14th September 1903 of a modification. The bayonets were modifications of the P88 bayonet in which the original crossguard and blade were mated with a new pommel and new grips held by two bolts. The new arms successfully passed their trials and production was authorised. The new bayonet was designated the **Sword Bayonet Pattern 1903** and consequently bears the pattern mark *1903* below the crown and royal cypher *E.R.*, (Edwardius Rex) of Edward VII, who reigned in the period 1901-10.

The straight double-edged blade, 305mm(12.00in) long, of the P88 was retained and left bright-polished except for about 6mm(0.25in) next to the crossguard which, like the guard and the hilt, was blued. The pommel returned to a more conventional style of beaked shape, an internal coil-spring press-stud positioned on the left and a T shaped bar attachment groove. The groove was easily cleaned by way of a cleaning hole drilled through the pommel at its end. The short guard has a 16.5mm(0.65in) muzzle ring and a small quillon. The whole bayonet measured 378mm(14.88in) overall and weighed 467gm (16.50oz). It was a well-balanced weapon when used either as a bayonet or as a knife, and its sharp double-edged blade made it effective in either cut or thrust.

Production of the P03 bayonets included the conversion of many P88 bayonets to the new specifications. This was easily accomplished, as it only necessitated replacing the pommel, machining the blade tang and fitting new grips. These converted bayonets have blades dated prior to 1903, together

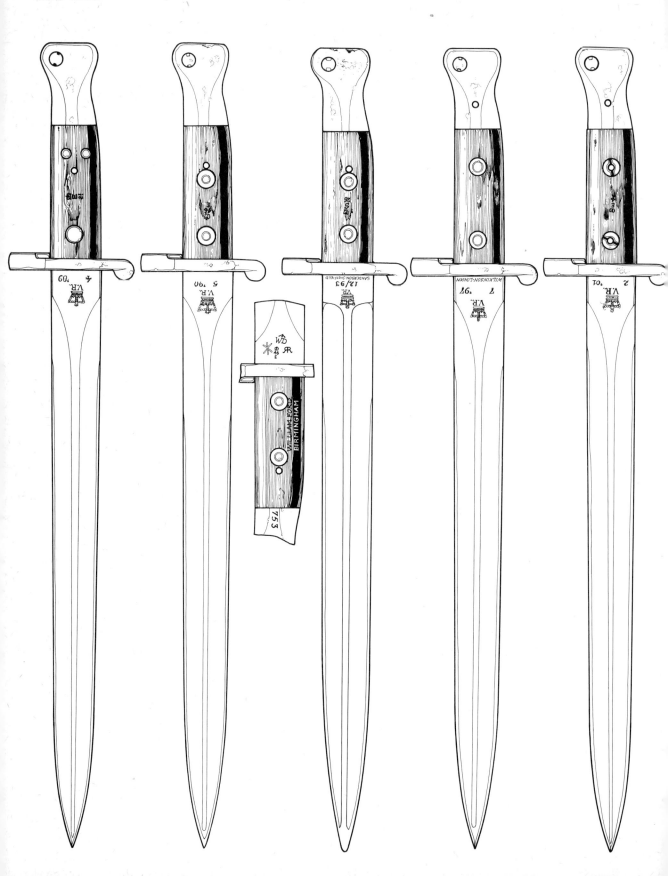

with the new markings. The manufacturers
responsible for the conversions also stamped their
initials on the top of the pommel. Thus a blade
marked *Wilkinson* might have the pommel stamped
EFD to show that it was converted at Enfield. Others
were altered and stamped *W.S.C.*, for the Wilkinson
Sword Company, or *R.F.I.* when they were converted
in India at the Rifle Factory Ishapore. The initials
S & N showed conversion by Sanderson Brothers
& Newbould of Sheffield.

The majority of P03 bayonets were made in the
period 1903-7 from new parts made by Wilkinson,
Sanderson, Mole and Enfield, or in India by RFI.
Many were issued with Pattern 1888 scabbards of one
type or another. The most common scabbard, leather
with a steel chape and a steel topmount with an oval
frog stud, was an earlier pattern originally designated
the **Scabbard, Sword Bayonet Pattern 1888 (Mk 1)
Land**. Pattern 1903 scabbards were, however,
manufactured and issued where stocks of existing P88
scabbards were insufficient. One was designed for the
army and another for the navy. The **Scabbard Pattern
1903 (Mk 1) Land** had a leather body, stitched at the
back, with an internal steel chape, only the tip of
which protruded; a steel topmount was enclosed
within the leather belt frog stapled at the back to the
body. This frog measured 140mm (5.50in) from the
mouthpiece, stitched for 69mm (2.72in) to form a
belt loop at the top. The overall length of the
scabbard, including the integral frog, was 464mm
(18.25in). The **Scabbard Pattern 1903 (Mk 3) Naval**
was identical to the land pattern with the exception
of the length of the belt frog, in which the loop was
much closer to the scabbard body and only measured
92mm (3.62in) from the mouthpiece giving the
scabbard an overall length of 16.50 in (419mm).

Though the P03 bayonet was made obsolescent by
the advent of the P07 bayonet, only four years after
its introduction, the outbreak of World War 1 and the
need to equip large armies meant that the P03
bayonet was again issued to many troops. It only
ended its active life in the British Army after World
War 2 in which it was often issued to Home Guard
and training units.

In India the extremes of heat and humidity often
damaged the leather scabbards and consequently
many of the Land Pattern examples used there were
reinforced by the addition of the steel end mounts of
the 1907 pattern.

51.   Sword bayonet, Pattern 1907

The **Sword Bayonet Pattern 1907** was introduced on
26th January 1907 along with the Rifle, Short,
Magazine Lee-Enfield Mark 3 (SMLE Mk 3), and was
the result of trials held with a variety of hybrid
designs utilising the best features of contemporary
foreign bayonets.

The weapon finally adopted owed much to the
Japanese 30th year bayonet of 1897, using a long
slim single-edged blade with a semi-spear point. The
steel guard was also fitted with a long swept forward
quillon, and the hilt was similar to that of the Pattern
1903 bayonet which had preceded the Pattern 1907
in service.

The 432mm (17.00in) blade gave the soldier a
greater reach than with the Pattern 1903, whose
blade was some 127mm (5.00in) shorter, and
compensated for the difference in length between the
various marks of the SMLE and the Long Lee Enfield
rifles. The shape of the P07, with its long single edge
sweeping up to the rounded back at the point, gave
an excellent cutting surface combined with an
efficient thrusting form. Long narrow fullers were
placed on each side to ease after-thrust withdrawal.
The blades were originally bright-finished, but during
World War 1 many were parkerised or sandblasted to
eliminate reflection from the polished surfaces.
Indian and Australian manufacturers preferred to
blue the blades for the same reason.

The hilts had plain wood grips secured by two
bolts, and the metal parts were blued. This blueing
was often overpainted khaki.

The swept forward quillon was found to have little practical use and was officially abandoned in 1913. At the same time it was ordered that the bayonets then in service were to have their quillons removed on the occasions when they were returned to store or for repair, but a considerable number escaped alteration—particularly those in the hands of the colonial troops that were rarely returned to store and which were generally repaired in the field. On 25th January 1916 a further modification was introduced by placing an oil and cleaning hole through the pommel, to be incorporated on all new production and to be added to the bayonets in service as and when they were returned. This, too, was often ignored and the Lithgow factory in Australia appears to have produced bayonets without this modification until 1920. The 'muzzle' ring was 17mm(0.659in) in diameter and fitted onto a round boss below the muzzle of the SMLE.

During the two wars many manufacturers produced the Pattern 1907, and their names and trademarks appeared on the blades close to the guard. In Britain the firms of Wilkinson Sword Company, Vickers-Armstrongs Limited, Robert Mole & Son, James A Chapman Limited, Sanderson Brothers & Newbould, and the Royal Small Arms Factory at Enfield Lock produced the bayonet, while America's Remington Arms Company supplied many to the British government. The Rifle Factory at Ishapore in India and the plant at Lithgow in Australia made large quantities; Australia's Orange Arsenal also made P07 bayonets during World War 2.

Apart from the finish, two minor manufacturing differences are worth noting; Vickers made their bayonets with a much larger oil hole than the others, while Mole's products have ricassos of different shape.

During World War 2 many P07 bayonets were sent to the Wilkinson factory for refurbishing. The hilts were painted black, the blades sandblasted and the date of reissue stamped on the ricassos. Actual production was limited in the period 1939-45 to Wilkinson, Ishapore and the Orange Arsenal in Australia. Those produced in India and Australia still used blueing as the final finish on both blade and hilt.

The first scabbard issued with the Pattern 1907 bayonet had a leather body stitched at the back, a steel topmount with a lozenge-shaped frog-stud and an internal chape of which only the metal tip protruded. This, the **Scabbard P07 Mk 1** was soon superseded by the **Scabbard P07 Mk 2** with an external steel chape. The mounts had curved edges where they met the leather and were secured by steel staples. The majority of later scabbards were produced with mounts that had straight edges and the frog stud was altered to an oval form. Many scabbards

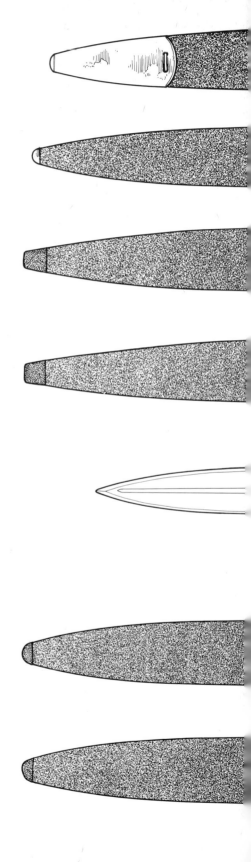

234-242

E.R.
1903
9 03

35 W

S.2.4
Y
C L D
21

WILKINSON LONDON

W 35

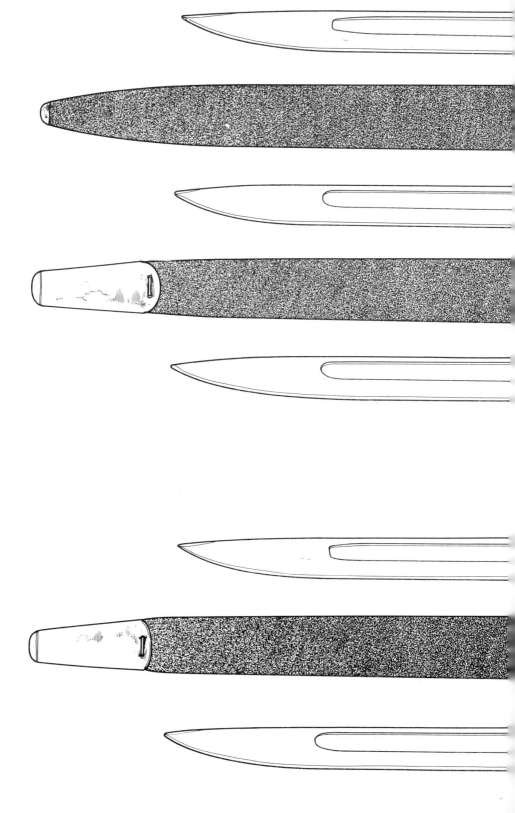

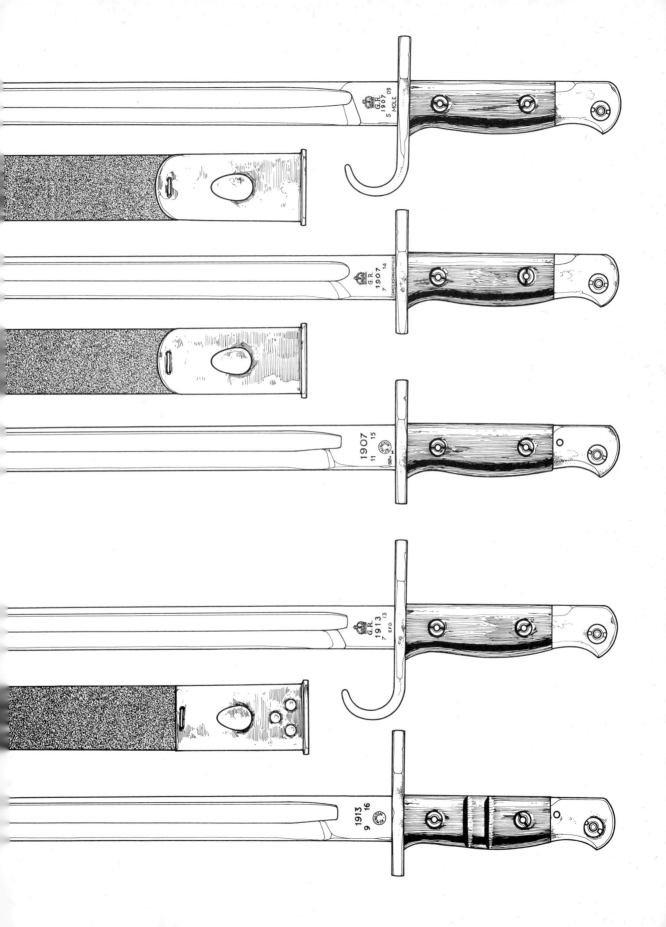

exist with a top mount of one type and a chape of another. During World War 1 Britain issued some scabbards experimentally which were made from two separate pieces of leather stitched together, with a raised seam at both back and front; these had the curved mounts that distinguish them from similar scabbards made in World War War 2 by the Australians, which had straight mounts.

With the exception of those bayonets made in Australia, all P07 bayonets had the pattern date of 1907 stamped on the blade ricasso below the crown and the monarch's cypher. The actual date of manufacture was stamped immediately below the pattern date, showing both month and year—'12 16' denoted December 1916—and below this (next to the crossguard) appeared the name or initials of the maker. Regimental markings were stamped on the pommel.

52.　Sword bayonet, Pattern 1913

Prior to the beginning of World War 1, the British Army was considering the adoption of a Mauser-type rifle to replace the SMLE. An experimental 0.276in(7mm) calibre rifle had been manufactured, but problems with the cartridge and its propellant (which eroded the bore too quickly and gave an excessive muzzle flash) prevented the plans from being finalised and the onset of the war caused them to be shelved.

The demands of the war, however, proved to be more than the factories making the SMLE could handle and so the experimental rifle was resurrected, converted to 0.303in calibre, and contracts for it were placed in America. The firms of Winchester and Remington (the latter using two plants, Ilion and Eddystone Arsenal) were the participants, and also made the bayonets.

The first **Sword Bayonet, Pattern 1913** was made in small numbers for the original 0.276in rifle and was virtually identical to the original quilloned Pattern 1907; the muzzle ring was, however, placed farther from the hilt to fit around the rifle's barrel. These bayonets and their rifles were made exclusively by RSAF Enfield Lock and carry the markings that

prove their authenticity; all were marked *EFD*, for Enfield, together with the month and year of manufacture, the royal cypher *G.R.,* and the pattern date '1913'. No oil holes were drilled into the pommels and the plain grips of the P07 were used.

The bayonets issued with the 0.303in Pattern 1914 rifle were the British **Sword Bayonet Pattern 1913** and the US **Bayonet M1917**. With the exception of a very small quantity of P13 bayonets made during 1915 by Vickers-Armstrong Limited, all were made in the USA by Remington or Winchester. As the P13 bayonet was adopted after the regulation declaring the quillon obsolete had been promulgated, none was ever manufactured with this device for catching an opponent's blade in close-quarter combat. The early P13 examples sent to Britain by the American makers were produced without the oil holes through the pommels, but a regulation of January 1916 instructed all manufacturers of British bayonets to add this alteration to new production. It also instructed armourers to modify those weapons in service when they were returned to store or for repair. It is possible, therefore, that a bayonet made in July 1915 may not have the oil hole possessed by one made in February 1915: many bayonets escaped the modification simply because they were never returned.

The actual dimensions of the P13 are essentially those of the P07, as the two shared the 432mm(17.00in) blade. The wood grips differ in that two deep grooves are cut across them to prevent confusion. The muzzle ring, of 15mm(0.591in) diameter, is placed further from the back of the hilt.

Most P13 bayonets were issued with British scabbards having a frog stud on the topmount, but some sent over in World War 2—under the terms of the Lend-Lease Programme—were equipped with the American scabbard which instead utilised the double hook attachment. These were carried in leather or webbing frogs which were prevented from slipping off by the hook attachment on top of the scabbard.

Owing to the American adoption of the M1917 bayonets (simply the P13 with different marks), and to the supply of M1917 bayonets to the British under the provisions of Lend-Lease, there can be a confusion of markings. This is complicated by American requisition of P13 bayonets, which bear dates prior to the adoption of the M1917; these bear no British marks and are instead stamped with standard US Army ones. The differences are summarised thus:

British P13 bayonets: standard British-style marks.
British P13 bayonets, requisitioned by the US Army at war's outbreak in 1917: no British marks, US marks, and dated earlier than 1917.
US M1917 bayonets: US marks with dates later than 1917.
US M1917 and requisitioned P13 bayonets supplied to Britain under the provisions of Lend-Lease: cancelled US marks and new British ones.

53.   Bayonet No 4

The Rifle No 4 Mk 1 was approved for issue on 15th November 1939, the result of trials first begun in the early 1920s. From an early stage it was decided that the long Pattern 1907 bayonet, which had been renamed Bayonet No 1 Mk 1 in 1926, was too long and unwieldy: the British had instead settled on a spike bayonet, the first of which had appeared with the Rifle No 1 Mk 6 in July 1925.

The spike bayonet was just that: it could be used for no other purpose, unlike the earlier sword bayonet which was also on occasion used for chopping wood and similar non-military tasks, and was designed purely and simply as a thrusting weapon. In this respect it was adequate, since tests held in 1922-4 had convinced the authorities that the short blade was capable of killing even the most thickly-clad enemy—who was taken to be a Russian in winter clothing. The spike was never popular with the troops, but it had the great advantage of the simplicity that made it easy to make; it was also very cheap, in terms of money, material and labour.

The **Bayonet No 4 Mk 1**, introduced on 15th November 1939, had a slender cruciform blade that tapered to a sharp point; the blade was a mere 200mm(7.88in) long and was attached to the hilt—or, more correctly, the socket—of which it was an integrally-forged part. Locking was effected by a longitudinally-sliding catch under the rear of the socket, which engaged with a lug on the rifle's muzzle. In this respect the Bayonet No 4 Mk 1 differed from the earlier experimental **Bayonet No 1 Mk 6,** of 1925 whose tubular catch slid laterally, although the two were otherwise very similar and used the same cruciform blade. The blade of the No 4 Mk 1 was bright-finished while the socket was blued.

The **Scabbard No 4 Mk 1,** issued with most of the various spike bayonets, was made of steel, tapering to end at the tip in a round ferrule and possessing a round frog-stud. A separate mouthpiece, made of

steel or zinc alloy, contained the blade-retaining springs and was held in place by two screws. The scabbards were either blued or painted black or khaki, depending on the theatre of operations for which they were intended.

The **Bayonet No 4 Mk 2**, introduced in 1940, was a wartime version of the Mk 1 in which further simplifications were made. On this model the blade was of circular section and tapered to a screwdriver point; it was made of a one-piece forging so that the blade and the socket were one. The blade consequently meets the socket with neither rim nor edge. Many of the Mk 2 bayonets were made under contract in the USA, and all are marked with the model designation and the name or trademark of the manufacturer (usually Stevens-Savage, whose mark was 5). Some of the blades were parkerised while others were blued, depending on the manufacturer's whim: the choice of either was theirs.

The **Bayonet No 4 Mk 2*** differed from the Mk 2 only in the method of manufacture, in which the blade and the socket were separate components welded or brazed together; there is thus a pronounced step where the blade meets the socket, although the two versions were otherwise identical. The Mk 2* was devised to permit bayonet production by firms who did not possess the equipment to forge the one-piece Mk 2.

In late 1942 the **Scabbard No 4 Mk 2** was approved, similar in construction to the Mk 1 scabbard but with parallel sides and ending in a flattened tip.

The final development of the spike bayonet was the **Bayonet No 4 Mk 3**, introduced on 12th February 1943 along with the third-pattern scabbard. The bayonet is sometimes known as the 'blacksmith's wonder'—a derisory term that aptly captures its appearance. Crudely welded of sheet-steel, without any attempts being made to clean the joints, the socket was of similar shape to the previous models and the circular-section blade was welded to it. The press-stud was also made of thin sheet-steel, and most weapons were heavily blued.

The **Scabbard No 4 Mk 3** was of plastic and used the same detachable mouthpiece as the other two types; the body, of black plastic, had a small oval frog-stud (also of plastic) and ended in a rounded tip through which a large drain-hole was cut.

The No 4 bayonets, apart from their use on the various No 4 rifles, were also issued with the Machine Carbine Sten Mk 5; the Mks 2 and 2* were produced in very large numbers, and are hence common, while the Mks 1 and 3 are more rarely seen.

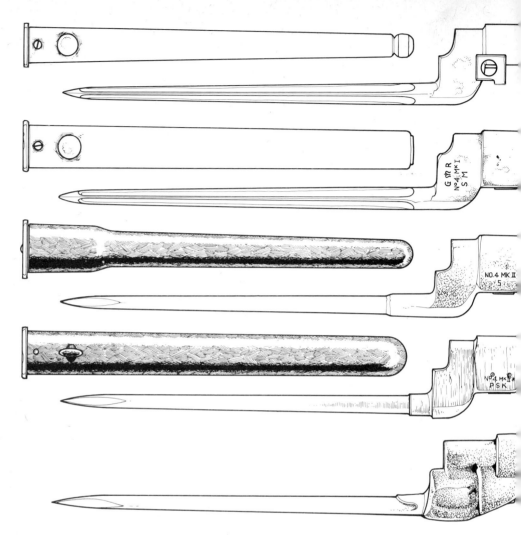

251 Scabbard No 4 Mk 1
252 Bayonet, experimental, for Rifle No 1 Mk 6
253 Scabbard No 4 Mk 2
254 Bayonet No 4 Mk 1
255 Scabbard No 4 Mk 2 by Victory Plastics
256 Bayonet No 4 Mk 2, by Stevens-Savage
257 Scabbard No 4 Mk 3
258 Bayonet No 4 Mk 2*, by Prince-Smith Limited of Keighley (Yorkshire)
259 Bayonet No 4 Mk 3

54. Bayonet No 5

World War 2 brought with it a request from the British troops fighting in the jungles of Burma for a shorter and lighter rifle to replace the Rifle No 1 and the Rifle No 4. The result was the Rifle No 5, introduced on 12th November 1944 but the design of which had been begun some two years earlier. The jungle carbine, fitted with a flash-hider and a rubber recoil pad to offset its light weight, was an excellent

weapon for use in close combat or conditions in which accuracy at long ranges was not the most important criterion. Following American practice a short bayonet, which could double as a general purpose knife, was also issued.

The design of the bayonet began towards the end of 1942, when the Armament Design Department at Cheshunt, after discussions with the Wilkinson Sword Company and others, produced the drawings for project **DD(E) SK1381** —a knife bayonet with a blade of 203mm (8.00in), the pommel of the Bayonet No 1 Mk 1 (and hence with a T-slot), and a blade of peculiar form. This weapon was found to leave much to be desired where ease of production was concerned, and so in mid-1943 a new bowie-type blade was adopted; by this time the project had been renamed **DD(E) 3640** and the T-slot had been changed to a O-slot.

The bayonet was accepted by the British Army in September 1944 and was completely different to any previous service pattern. A bowie blade is used with its characteristic single edge sweeping up to a double-edged point, and the blade back is rounded; a deep square fuller, 136mm(5.38in) long, appears on each side. The carbine even had a flash-hider to avoid giving too clear an indication of the firer's position, but the bayonet blade was finished bright, although the hilt and the guard were blackened.

The crossguard features a large muzzle ring with the diameter of 22.5mm(0.886in), which fits over the flared flash-hider; the lower guard has a hole drilled through it and there is an example of a thick wire knuckle-guard in the Imperial War Museum which slots into this hole and into the bar attachment groove.

The plain wood grips are secured by either one or two bolts, but contrary to popular belief there is no distinction officially drawn between the 'No 5 Mk 1' and the 'No 5 Mk 2', regardless of the fact that the Wilkinson Sword Company (whose suggestion led to the addition of the second bolt) drew such a distinction in their records. To differentiate between the two variations the first (one bolt) has been called the **Bayonet No 5 Mk 1 first pattern**, and the second (two bolts) the **Bayonet No 5 Mk 1 second pattern**. The grips completely cover the tang.

The steel pommel has an oil drainage hole and the round press-stud face that protrudes from the obverse or right side is slotted to make removal possible with a screwdriver. The bar attachment groove is round and accepts the carbine's attachment bar which is part of the foresight protector. This swells to a spherical tip which slides at right angles into the groove, where the press-stud locks it in position. The hilt is shaped to fit the hand and the bayonet has an overall length of 302mm(11.88in).

The Bayonet No 5 was declared obsolete for the jungle carbine in 1947, when the gun's specific purpose had been fulfilled; the bayonet, however, was retained for use on the Sterling machine carbine. These specimens, which do not have oil drainage holes in the pommels, were originally provided with wood grips on which the word *Sterling* was impressed; those of newer production have black plastic grips held in place by two steel rivets. They are officially known as **Bayonets, Sterling submachine-gun, L2A1**.

The all-steel blackened scabbards have round frog-studs and drainage holes cut in their tips. They were carried in webbing frogs, but are rarely found with obsolete bayonets—having been retained for use with newer types of bayonet.

55.   Bayonets No 7 and No 9

Towards the end of the war, no doubt influenced by the criticism of the spike bayonets voiced by the troops in the field, the British authorities decided to develop a knife bayonet. This, it was noted, required a socket of some pattern to enable it to fit the No 4 rifle (which would have otherwise needed modifications made to it) and it was also decided to use the blade of the Bayonet No 5 Mk 1, which had then just entered production. In the summer of 1944 representatives of the Royal Small Arms Factory at Enfield Lock, of the Armament Design Department at Cheshunt, of the Wilkinson Sword Company and of others met to discuss the weapon, and the result was **Bayonet DDE(SK) 1475** (the figures refer to the drawing number). This was a strange and very complicated marriage of the locking mechanism of the No 4 spike bayonets with the blade of the No 5, and the whole was given a hilt of Tufnel—plastic-impregnated cloth—through which ran a longitudinal hole for the passage of the bullet. The hilt was raised above the blade and a rudimentary guard was brazed to the tang, but the result was very complex and awkward in the hand and so the project was dropped after no more than a handful of bayonets had been made.

The second project, **Bayonet DD(E) 1475**, consisted of the No 5 blade mated with a standard type of hilt to which a raised socket was added at the pommel. Although this weapon was a more satisfactory weapon from a manufacturing viewpoint, the protruding pommel-socket gave a very uncomfortable handgrip and the lack of a satisfactory crossguard was also criticised. The project was also dropped after no more than ten prototypes had been made, and the designers instead developed the Bayonet No 7 in which the idea of DD(E) 1475 was modified by the addition of a crossguard and a swivelling socket.

The **Bayonet No 7** was introduced on a limited scale in 1946, but only the Guards and a few other selected units ever received it. The 200mm(7.88in) blade was that of the No 5 jungle carbine bayonet, and the No 5 crossguard was used without alteration—although its purpose was not to support the bayonet on the rifle, owing to the fact that the rifle barrel did not protrude past the pommel-socket. The large-diameter muzzle ring of the No 5 bayonet permitted passage of the bullet through it and ensured that stock components could be used wherever possible. The socket was of similar design to that of the Mk 1, Mk 2 and 2* spike bayonets, but it could be rotated into one of two positions and locked there by a spring-loaded sliding catch. In the 'stowed' or *down* position the socket acted as an extension of the Tufnel grips, whereupon the bayonet could be used as a knife; in the 'open' or *up* position the socket stood above the back of the hilt and could be fitted to the rifle.

All the metal parts were heavily blacked with the exception of the blade, which was left bright-finished. The grips, made of Tufnel (plastic-impregnated cloth) were held to the tang by two bolts and varied in colour from black to red, orange or brown. The scabbard issued was that of the No 5.

The **Bayonet No 9 Mk 1** (no other marks were ever issued) was a combination of the No 5 blade with a simple fixed socket based on that of the No 4 spike bayonets. The blade, which measured 205mm(8.13in), was bright-finished with the exception of the last 13mm(0.50in) nearest the scabbard, which—like the socket and the scabbard body—was heavily blacked. The socket was stamped *No.9 Mk1* together with the War Department broad arrow and the manufacturer's code number.

The steel scabbard is that of the Nos 5 and 7. The Royal Navy was issued with the majority of the No 9 bayonets, as it kept the No 4 rifle after the army had been issued with the semiautomatic L1A1. The No 7 and the No 9, owing to the fact that they fitted the No 4 rifle, could also be used with the Sten Mk 5 machine carbine.

56. Bayonets L1A1 and L1A3

In 1957 the British Army adopted the L1A1 semiautomatic rifle, a modified version of Fabrique Nationale's Fusil Automatique Léger (light automatic rifle), and at the same time the opportunity was taken to introduce a new universal system of classification in which the prefix letter L represented land service, N was naval service, and A stood for air service: this was followed by the pattern number, by the letter A, and then by the modification number.

The first bayonet to be introduced was the **Bayonet L1A1**, based on the Canadian **Bayonet C1** introduced in 1955; the Canadians were the first country (excluding Belgium) to mass-produce the FN rifle, manufacture of which was begun at their Longbranch Arsenal in June 1955. The blade of the L1A1 is 203mm(8.00in) long, single-edged with a 64mm(2.50in) false edge, and curves to a bowie-type point. The blade has deep fullers, each some 140mm(5.50in) long, while the steel crossguard has a muzzle ring of 15mm(0.591in) diameter and a small hole of 6mm (0.24in) diameter in the lower part of the guard. The pommel has a press stud that is operated by an internal spring, and the stud protrudes some distance from the pommel—which provides a way of distinguishing the L1A1 from the later L1A3. All these bayonets, without exception, were issued with pressed-steel grips held by two deeply-sunk rivets. The grips are stamped *L1A1* together with the NATO stores number *9600011* and the War Department's broad arrow. The Canadian C1 bayonet differs from the L1A1 principally in the less pronounced and shorter bowie point.

The **Bayonet L1A3** (the experimental L1A2 was never produced in quantity) is identical to the L1A1 with the exception of the press stud design, which was modified to prevent the bayonet being knocked from the rifle by an accidental blow on the catch: something which apparently happened with the L1A1. The press-stud was much shortened so that it lay almost flush with the hilt, and the surround was cut away so that the stud could be depressed into the side of the hilt. These bayonets are similarly marked to the L1A1: the grips are marked *L1A3 9600257*, together with the War Department mark, and occasionally the Enfield monogram Ð followed by two figures representing the year of manufacture. Later examples have a modified crossguard with straight sides.

Some L1A1 bayonets have been modified to L1A3 standards and can be easily recognised by their markings: the grips are stamped *L1A1*, but the end of the pommel is stamped *L1A3/0257*. The most recent L1A3 bayonets, at the time of writing, have the modified press-stud, a straight-sided crossguard, and a new pattern of blade in which the fullers are only 102mm(4.00in) long; it was found difficult to

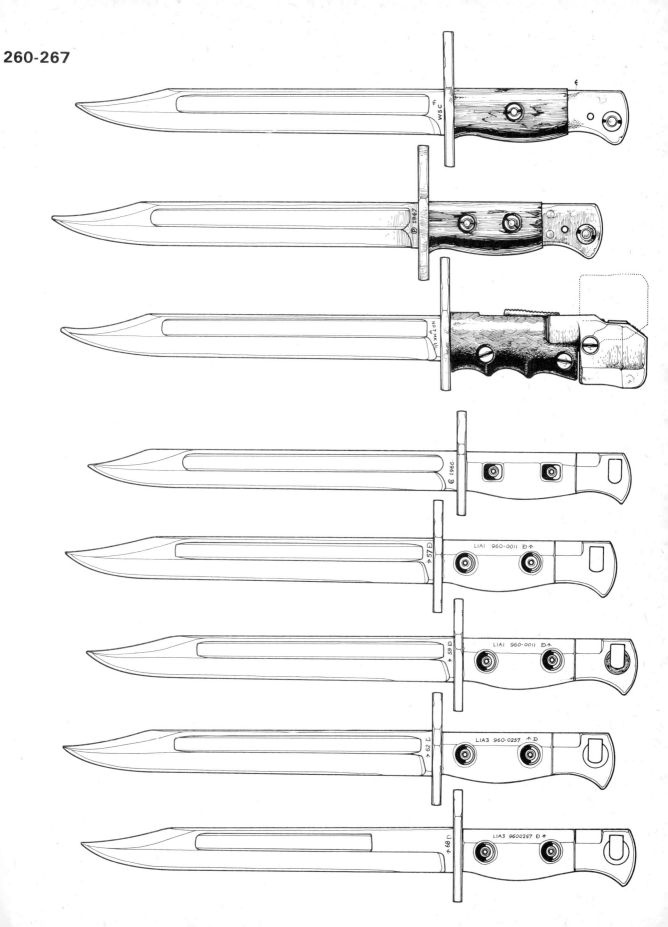

successfully heat-temper the blade shoulders when the long fullers so closely approached the guard. The short fullers end 35mm(1.38in) from the guard, and effectively cure the fault.

All these bayonets have the steel scabbards used on all British bowie-blade types and they are carried in web frogs—except on parade when white buff-leather or, more recently, white plastic frogs are issued. The blades are parkerised or bright-finished, while the other metal parts are painted black. Following recent trials, a plastic scabbard has been approved but it is not yet (1973) in issue.

United States of America

57. Sword and knife bayonets, 1905–1943

The US Army's bayonet development rarely followed the contemporary trends evident in Europe, owing to a combination of geographic insularity and an entirely different set of localised design criteria. Thus the Board of Ordnance had long been keen on the rod bayonet, despite the fact that most European armies had long discarded such weapons on account of their fragility.

The experiments to find a replacement for the Krag-Jørgensen rifles, then in the US Army, led to the adoption in 1901 of a Mauser-type rifle known as the *US Magazine Rifle, Caliber. 30, M1901.* This was in turn developed into the 1903 short rifle, approximately 95000 of which were produced with **Rod Bayonets M1903** in the period from 19th June 1903 to the beginning of 1905. The inefficiency of the rod bayonet was then conclusively demonstrated by Theodore Roosevelt, President of the USA, and a knife bayonet was designed instead; the result was the **Bayonet Model 1905**, recommended for adoption on 28th March by the General Staff, the acceptance order for which was signed by Taft (Secretary of War) on 3rd April 1905. It was noted at the time that the bayonet was not to be issued to the cavalry, who carried revolvers for close-quarter combat.

Production of the M1905 bayonet began at Springfield Armory and Rock Island Arsenal in 1906 and continued until 1922 and 1918/19 respectively. During World War 2, however, the bayonet was introduced under the designation **Bayonet Model 1942** with but minor modifications—the principal of which was the substitution of plastic grips for those of wood. At the same time many original M1905 specimens were regripped, while manufacture of the M1942 was divided amongst many private firms.

Thus, with a single modification, the basic design of the M1905 served the US Army through two world wars.

The M1905 is a conventional sword bayonet with a blade of 405mm(16.00in), fullers, and a double-edged spear point; the attachment method, however, is a most interesting adaptation of the original Norwegian Krag pattern of 1894. The Americans rejected the German-pattern internal coil-spring mechanism used by most other nations, despite the fact that they had themselves used the standard press-stud on their M1892 (Krag) knife bayonet. It must be noted that there are advantages and disadvantages in both.

The release catch is situated on the underside of the hilt behind the guard, where it bears on an extension bar contained within the hilt which in turn acts as the lock for the rifle's T-lug. The tip of the extension bar protrudes from the base of the bayonet's attachment slot until pressure on the guard catch depresses it. The guard of the M1905 also possesses two slots, one above and one below the blade, which mate with hooks on the scabbard mouthpiece to hold the bayonet in place. The release catch also acts as a release for the scabbard lock. In all other respects the bayonet is conventional in design, with a beaked steel pommel and slightly-ridged wood grips; those grips of wartime manufacture were sanded smooth. The diameter of the guard's muzzle ring is 15.7mm(0.618in). Earliest examples of the bayonet have blued hilts with bright-finished blades, but after the United States' entry into World War 1 the blades were first blued and then parkerised to give a non-reflective finish.

Four different scabbards were issued with the M1905. The first **Scabbard M1905** had a leather body, a steel mouthpiece and a steel belt loop attached to the back of the body and permitted a degree of oscillation (50°). The second **Scabbard M1905** was similar, but with a longer topmount; the belt attachment remained the same. These scabbards were later modified, after c.1910/12, by removing the swivelling belt loop and replacing it with a leather loop—stitched around the topmount—which held a bent-wire double hook that engaged two eyelets in the belt. The most widely issued scabbard used during World War 1 was the **Scabbard M1910**, which has a hide body completely covered by a loose canvas cover with a leather tip: the double-hook belt attachment was used.

By 1942 the US Cavalry Board felt that the long M1905 and M1942 bayonets were too long for many troops, especially those still on horseback or in vehicles. They consequently decided to shorten existing bayonets by removing the last 152mm(6.00in) of the blades and reshaping the points. The experimental bayonet, known during its development as the **Bayonet M1905E1**, was standardised in March 1943 as the **Bayonet M1**. Two types of point exist, one a simple copy of the original and the other a hatchet type. New M1 bayonets were then produced by the factories that had been making the M1942 and can be recognised by the short-fullered blades. The scabbards issued were originally shortened **Scabbards M3**; the M3 has been designed in 1940 by the Beckwith Manufacturing Company and was first produced in 1942 for the M1942. It has an olive drab plastic-reinforced cloth body, with a steel topmount and the double-hook attachment. Some bayonets were issued with the essentially similar **Scabbard, Navy, Mark 1** which was originally intended for training bayonets. Later bayonets used the **Scabbard M7**, really no more than a newly-made short M3.

All M1905 bayonets are similarly marked. The arsenal's initials—*S.A.* for Springfield Armory or *R.I.A.* for Rock Island Arsenal—were stamped on the reverse ricasso above the Board of Ordnance and Fortification's 'flaming bomb' mark and the year of manufacture. The obverse ricasso bears the letters *U.S.* and the bayonet serial number. M1942 bayonets, more crudely made than the M1905 type, are stamped with the maker's initials (for example *UFH* for the Union Fork & Hoe Company), the 'flaming bomb' the letters *U.S.* and the date: all appeared on the reverse ricasso. M1 bayonets bore similar markings to those of the M1942.

58. Sword bayonet, 1917

The service rifle of the US Army, on its entry in 1917 into World War 1, was the *Rifle, Cal .30, M1903*—the 'Springfield'. The rapid expansion of the armed forces, however, rapidly outstripped production of the M1903 rifle and so the ordnance authorities were forced to find alternative sources of supply. A solution was found by purchasing quantities of the British P14, then being manufactured in three American factories, whose design was easily altered to handle the standard .30 M1906 cartridge; the result was known as the *Rifle, Cal .30, M1917*. No alteration of the external barrel diameter was necessary and hence the original P14 bayonets were used. The first batches of bayonets were requisitioned from stocks intended for Britain and these consequently have the US Ordnance marks stamped over the cancelled British ones—and hence are easily identifiable. The stamps include the cancelled pattern stamp *1913*, together with the date of manufacture (*ie* '8 16' for August 1916) and the manufacturer's name. On the obverse or right side of the blade can be found the War Department broad arrow and inspection marks, overstamped with the letters *U.S.* and the 'flaming bomb' mark of the US Ordnance Department.

M1917 bayonets of new production are stamped *1917* on the reverse ricasso together with the maker's name or mark. The Remington Arms Company marked their name in full—*Remington* within a

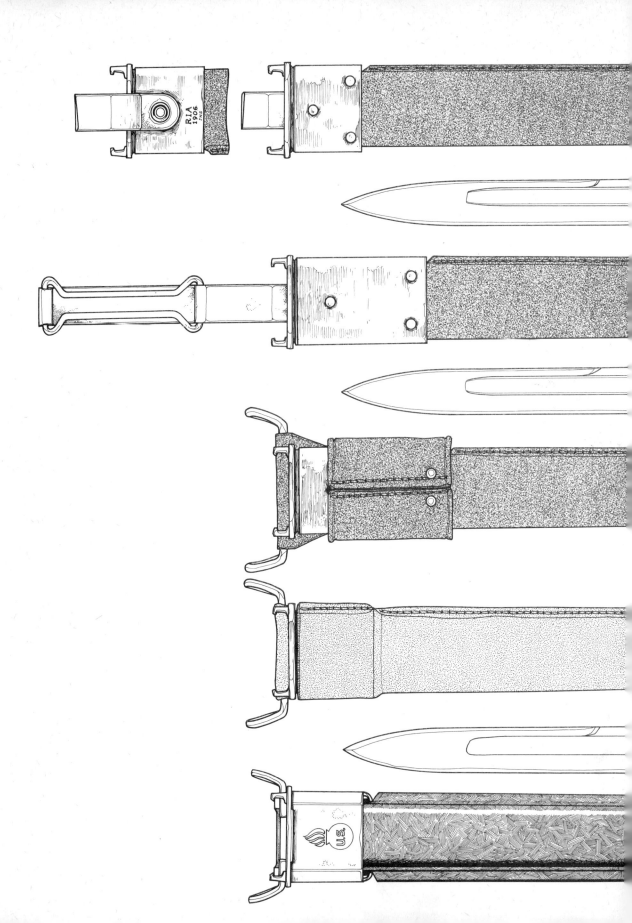

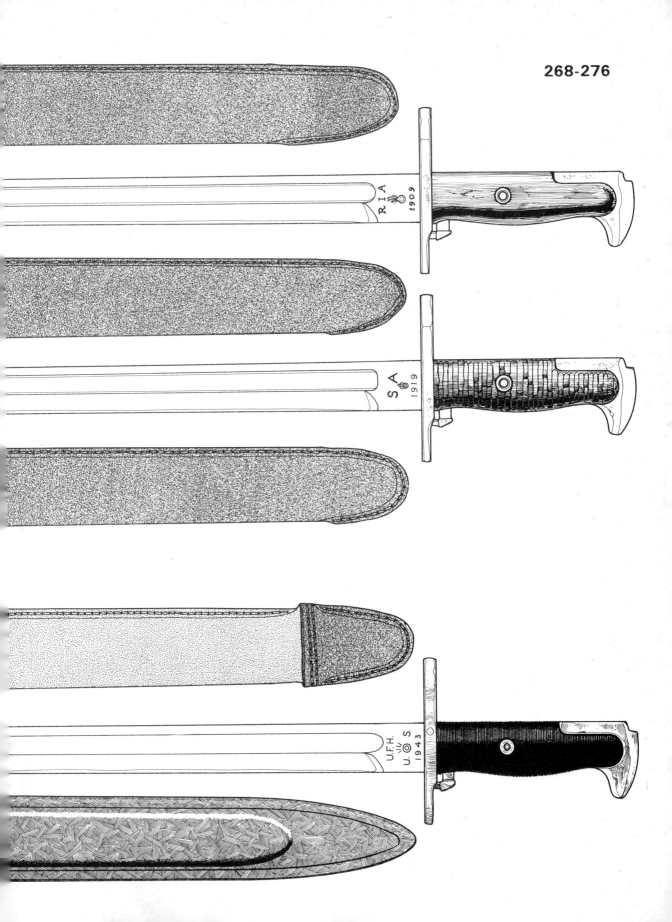

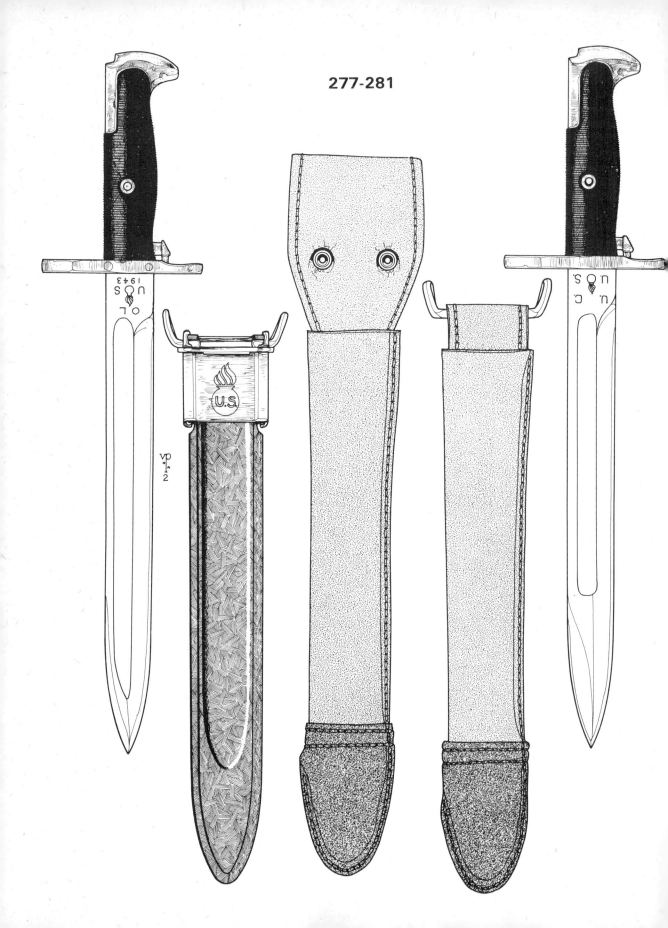

277-281

circle—while the Winchester Repeating Arms Company used only the initial *W,* sometimes encircled. The 'flaming bomb' ordnance mark, together with the letters *U.S.,* appeared on the reverse. The ex-British bayonets possessed both the pattern year (1913) and the month and year of manufacture, but the American M1917 had only the year of completion: thus the few bayonets completed in 1918 bear this date instead of 1917.

These bayonets have the 432mm (17.00in) straight single-edged blade originally designed for the British Pattern 1907. The hilts are also very similar but the muzzle rings, of 15.5mm (0.610in) diameter, are placed further from the back of the hilt. The crossguard is therefore longer. The wood grips, held by two bolts, had two deep grooves cut across their width: these not only improved grip but—more important—prevented confusion with the Pattern 1907. Some blades were finished bright while others were blued or parkerised.

Three American scabbards were issued with the Model 1917 bayonets, two during World War 1 and the third during World War 2. The first was similar to the British type, with a leather body and steel mounts, but instead of a frog-stud the topmount had a metal block on the back to which a leather holder was attached by two rivets. A brass wire double-hook attachment was held by the leather loop and enabled it to be carred in two small holes in the belt. The second scabbard differed in that the wire hook attachment was held by an extension of the topmount's mouthpiece. In most cases the complete scabbard was painted olive drab.

In 1944 a plastic-reinforced cloth scabbard was introduced to conform to the scabbards then being issued with the Models 1905 and 1942. This had an olive drab body with a steel mouthpiece incorporating the double-hook attachment and were stamped *U.S. M.1917* and *B.M.CO.* The Beckwith Manufacturing Company produced 179000 of these scabbards for use with the M1917 bayonets still in use with the National Guard and the navy.

59.   Bayonet-knife M4

The M3, a general-purpose knife, is included here because the M4 bayonet was its direct descendant; between 1943 and 1944 some 2 500 000 of these knives were produced to fill the need for a hand-to-hand weapon for those troops not equipped with bayonets. At the time the M3 was introduced, the bulk of the American forces were armed either with the Rifle M1 (Garand) or the Rifle M1903A 1 or M1903A3 (Springfield), all of which were issued with the rather heavy M1905, M1942 or M1 designs of bayonet. The M3 was an important weapon, light and well-balanced, and though intended as a completely different weapon to the issue bayonets its importance lies in that it provided the base for the M4 and all American postwar bayonet development.

The blade chosen for the M3 was a partially double-edged type in which one edge was sharpened for its length while the other extended only some 89mm(3.50in) from the point; the blade's length was 172mm(6.75in). The hilt was made from six leather washers placed over the blade tang, which gave the impression of an all-leather grip grooved to afford a better grip. These were held in place by a steel pommel, and the upward extension of the steel crossguard was swept forward to permit better purchase for the thumb. The entire knife weighs only some 255gm(9.00oz). The original M6 scabbard was ultimately replaced by the M4 bayonets' M8 and M8A1 patterns.

The manufacturer's name occasionally appears on the blade, and in some cases so too does the date—for example *US M3 Imperial 1943,* manufactured by the Imperial Cutlery Company, or *US M3 Kinfolks Inc.* The majority, however, was stamped on the straight part of the crossguard with the designation *US M3* together with all or part of the manufacturer's name, which could be *Case* (W R Case & Sons, Bradford, Pennsylvania), *Pal* (Pal Blade & Tool Company, Plattsburg, New York), *Utica* (Utica Cutlery

282-285

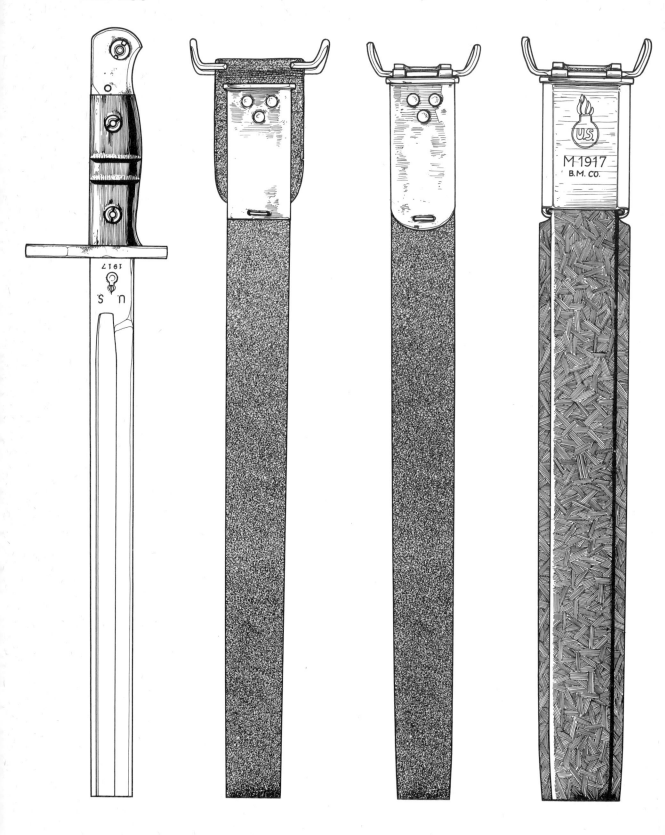

Company, Utica, New York), *Boker* (Hermann Boker & Company, New York), *Camillus* (Camillus Cutlery Company, New York) or *K.I.* (Kinfolks Incorporated). Those knives sold through retail stores, both during and after the war, always had the markings removed from the guard.

As the Carbine M1 came into use during 1944, a new bayonet was required to fit it. The M3 knife had become extremely popular, especially in the Pacific Theater, and so it was modified to fit the carbine, providing the troops with both a bayonet and a utility knife. In July 1944 the **Bayonet-knife M4** was approved, and production of the M3 was discontinued in the following month. The blade and grip of the M3 were retained by the M4, but a new crossguard with a 15mm(0.578in) diameter muzzle ring was added. The plain steel pommel of the M3 was replaced by a version in which was cut a small bar-attachment groove and in which there were two spring-loaded pivoting locking catches. The heavier pommel, unfortunately, destroyed many of the M3's pleasant handling characteristics. Most of the M3 manufacturers also produced the M4 bayonet and stamped the crossguard with their marks, *U.S. M4*, and in some cases with the ordnance department's 'flaming bomb'. In addition several other makers—*A.C.C.* (American Cutlery Company, Chicago and New York), *Aerial* (Aerial Machine & Tool Company, New York) and *TMN* (unknown)—also made the M4, which was issued with either the M8 or the M8A1 scabbard.

As the war progressed a fault became evident in the leather grips, in which the washer nearest the guard rotted as a result of the Pacific's humidity. This lower washer was consequently often replaced by one of a water-resistant resin compound, slightly altering the grip's shape.

A crudely-chequered wood grip was used to replace some rotted leather grips and these are usually also fitted with brown plastic spacers at each end, protecting the steel pommel and crossguard from the humidity which might otherwise accelerate rusting. Some hilts were even replaced by a moulded one-piece rubber pattern, with the same six grooves as the leather-washer pattern; these are particularly rare

and are thought to have been little more than experimental.

In 1956—after all attempts to prevent mildew, fungus and rot had failed—new plastic grips were adopted for the last of the M4 bayonets. These are in two pieces held to the tang by two slotted-head bolts, and the surface is finely chequered to improve the handgrip.

All the metal surfaces of the M4 were parkerised, and the scabbards (made of cloth impregnated with an olive-drab plastic) were originally issued with a leather thong which passed through an eyelet on the scabbard tip and around the wearer's thigh, securely holding the scabbard in place.

60. Bayonet-knives, M5, M6 and M7

The **Bayonet-Knife M5** was adopted in 1955 for use on the Rifle M1 (Garand) and the various alterations of the rifle that were then in service. The blade is identical to that of the M4 but the method of attaching the bayonet to the rifle is very different; the crossguard has no muzzle ring, but instead a backward-facing steel button attached to the upper part of the guard. This engages a hole in the gas-cylinder lock-plug under the muzzle of the rifle, and serves the same purpose as the muzzle ring would otherwise have done: it together with the catch, provides a means of holding the bayonet securely in place.

The hilt is of conventional shape with a straight flat back and a shaped lower edge that fits the hand; the pommel has a standard bar-attachment groove, but the catch (unlike the twin sprung arms of the M4) is based upon that of the original Norwegian m/1894 Krag-Jørgensen bayonet which provided the prototype—so far as the locking mechanism was concerned—for the American M1905, M1942 and M1 bayonets. It consists of a pivoted catch operated by a long stud lever whose end protrudes below the hilt at the guard. The grips of the M5 are of black plastic and the greater part of the surface is chequered.

286   Knife M3, by Imperial Cutlery Company, c.1942/3
287   Obverse blade of 286
288   Bayonet-knife M4, by Camillus Cutlery Company, leather grips
289   Bayonet-knife M4 by American Cutlery Company, moulded rubber grip
290   Bayonet-knife M4, by Pal Blade and Tool Company, plastic grips
291   Dutch version of the M4, made in 1951/2 by E & F Hörster of Solingen
292   Bayonet-knife M5 (guard detail)
293   Bayonet-knife M6

286-293

US M3 IMPERIAL

US M4
CAMILUS

US M4
O.A.C.C

US M4
PAL

The bayonet is stamped on the face of the guard with the maker's name or initials, together with the legend *U.S. M5*; all the metal parts are parkerised. The M5, the last bayonet to be issued with the Garand, is now to be found throughout the South American countries supplied with old American weapons under the various agreements and aid programmes of the 1960s. Owing to the unique attachment method, the M5 holds a special place in the story of bayonet design.

In 1957 the USA adopted a new 7.62mm rifle known as the M14, which was intended to replace not only the Rifle M1 (Garand) but also the Browning Automatic Rifle M1918A2, the Submachine-gun M3A1 and the Carbines M1 and M2. The unique attachment device of the M5 could not be readily adapted to fit the Rifle M14, and so the crossguard was reinstated on the **Bayonet-Knife M6** although the rest of the locking mechanism remained unchanged. The diameter of the ring is 20mm(0.787in), the large size of which is necessary to fit over the rifle's flash suppressor. The length and design of the blade was that of the M4, and the blade and the metal parts were all parkerised a dull-grey matt finish, which was both non-reflective and rustproof. The face of the guard bears the manufacturer's name or initials and the mark *U.S. M6.*

The bayonet's hilt is almost identical to that of the earlier M5 and, if necessary, most of the internal parts can be interchanged; the black grips have chequering that is both more clearly defined and more deeply cut than that of the M5. The border of the chequering is also more clearly defined that that of the older model. At the time the M6 was adopted a considerable lobby arose to abolish the bayonet completely, but the fact that the army had designed its bayonets to act also as utility knives swayed the case and the bayonet remained. The M6, in fact, weighs a mere 325gm(11.5oz), making it light enough to permit accurate firing with a fixed bayonet; it is also relatively well-balanced when used in the hand.

The various jungle campaigns undertaken by the US Army in the Far East—especially Vietnam—convinced many that lighter and more handy rifle was needed. The result was the introduction of the Stoner-designed Armalite AR15 light automatic rifle, whose calibre was a mere 5.56mm(0.223in), which was adopted after trials as the Rifle M16; the present weapon, the M16A1, is but a minor modification in which a bolt-closing device has been added. In addition to the American usage of this weapon, some have been supplied to the British Army for trials in such places as Malaysia, while others have been sold to Australia (for use in Vietnam) and to South Vietnam itself.

The two bayonets issued with the small-calibre rifle, the **Bayonet-Knife AR15** and the **Bayonet-Knife M7**, combine the locking mechanism and blade of the M4 with the large-diameter muzzle ring of the M6.

The AR15 bayonet, Colt's prototype, resembles the old M4 except that the design is generally lighter and that the grips are of olive-drab plastic-grooved and ridged in old M4 style. The grips may be found painted mid-blue, for the AR15 was initially used by the USAF before being adopted by the army. The parkerised blade is stamped *Colts Pt. F.A. Mfg. Co. Hartford Ct. U.S.A.* in a single line. The scabbards were of unmarked M8 type.

The M7 differs from the Colt bayonet in that the grips are of chequered black plastic held by two bolts. The only markings found on this bayonet are the designation *U.S. M7* on the face of the guard and *Milpar* (the tradename of the Columbus Milpar and Manufacturing Company Inc, of Columbus in Ohio). The bayonets are issued with the M8A1 scabbard.

All bayonets of the M5/M6/M7 series are issued with the M8 or M8A1 scabbards, the latter an improvement over the former sanctioned in 1958. The scabbards are of plastic-impregnated cloth, with webbing frogs with loops and press-fasteners to hold the bayonet securely in the scabbard. They are fixed to the belt by means of a wire hook assembly and most are drilled with a small hole in the tip—officially a drain hole, but often used to take a leather thong that was then used to tie the tip of the scabbard to the wearer's thigh. Some newer M8A1 scabbards are to be found with metal tip reinforces with eyelets, through which the tie-down thong can be passed.

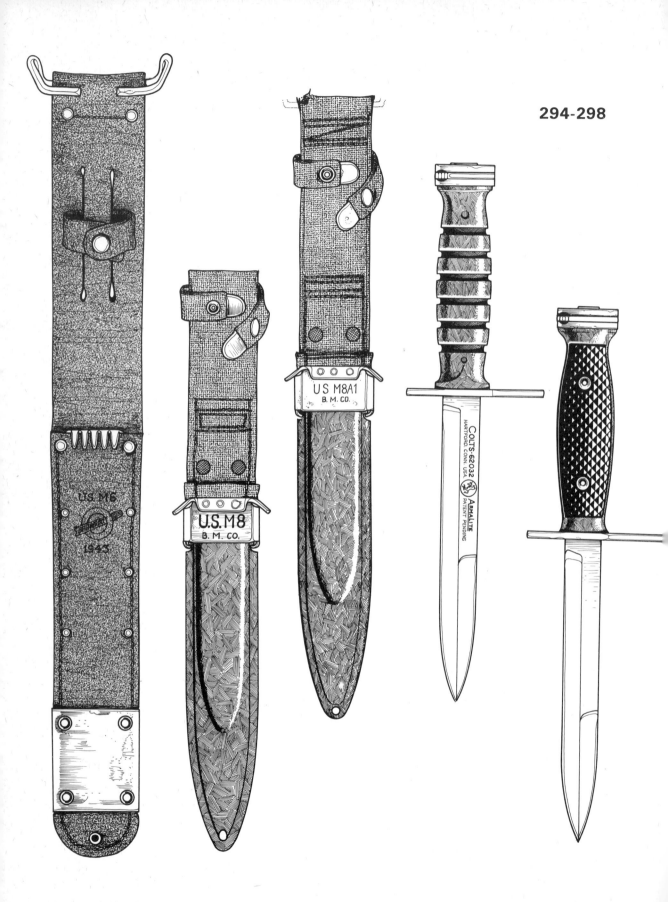

294-298

U.S. M6
1943

U.S. M8
B. M. CO.

US M8A1
B. M. CO.

COLTS-62032
HARTFORD, CONN. U.S.A.
ARMALITE
PATENT PENDING

Appendices

British and Commonwealth bayonet markings

The Pattern 1907 bayonet, redesignated No 1 Mk 1 in 1926, was produced in millions from 1907-45, issued to all Empire and Commonwealth troops and—even when obsolete—sold to many other nations. It has been used by more countries and in more conflicts than any other bayonet: its 17in(432mm) blade, plain wood grips and steel hilt can still be seen on the parade grounds of many countries in Africa and the East.

Most countries of the British Empire were issued with bayonets produced and sent out from Britain. These differed from the British bayonets only in their markings, for the country's acceptance mark was usually stamped on the bayonet's pommel. The majority was issued during World War 1 and clearly marked as illustrated. Marks **1** and **2** were used by Canada, **4** by South Africa, **5** shows the early Australian Department of Defence marking superseded by **6**, **7** was New Zealand's marking and **8** that of India.

While most of the Empire relied on Britain for their supplies, both India and Australia produced the Pattern 1907 in their own factories. The Indians started production as early as September 1907 at the Rifle Factory Ishapore; the marking of RFI thus appears on the blade's ricasso below the actual date of manufacture and the initials GRI (for Georgius Rex Imperator) below the Imperial crown. The India Government mark, **9**, together with **8**, appears on the opposite ricasso. Australia, while accepting many ex-British bayonets into service, also manufactured the Pattern 1907 throughout both wars. Those made during World War 1 have the arsenal's name of Lithgow stamped in full below the date of manufacture. Later examples, made during World War 2, were stamped with **13** (for Orange Arsenal) or **14** (for Munitions Australia). The wood grips were stamped by the maker, Slazenger, with an abbreviation of their name—SLAZ—together with the date of manufacture.

During World War 1 Australia was divided into military districts, and so bayonets used or issued to troops raised in these areas had the crossguard and scabbard mouthpiece stamped with the district's number and the arm's serial number. A bayonet from Victoria, for example, could be stamped 3.M.D.24891, showing that it was from the 3rd Military District Command, weapon serial number 24891. The districts were as follows:

1.M.D.: Queensland
2.M.D.: New South Wales
3.M.D.: Victoria which included the separate command of Tasmania
4.M.D.: South Australia
5.M.D.: Western Australia

The bayonets made in Britain carried the manufacturer's name or trademark on the blade ricasso.

Chapman or JAC: James A Chapman & Son, Sheffield, Yorkshire
Enfield or EFD: Royal Small Arms Factory, Enfield Lock, Middlesex
Mole: Robert Mole & Son, Birmingham
Remington (often encircled): Remington Arms Company, Ilion, New York
Sanderson: Sanderson Brothers & Newbould, Sheffield, Yorkshire
Vickers: Vickers-Armstrong Limited, Crayford, Kent
Wilkinson or Wilkinson Pall Mall: Wilkinson Sword Company, London (World War 1)
WSC S 294: Wilkinson Sword Company, London (World War 2)

Two other markings were used; **11** is the naval acceptance mark and **12** the 'Drill Purpose' mark usually encountered on weapons with blunted points.

During World War 2 the No 4 Mk 2 spike bayonet, together with the No 4 rifle, replaced many of the older SMLE rifles and their P07 bayonets. These bayonets were also manufactured abroad as well as in Britain. Canadian bayonets were produced at their Long Branch Arsenal, **3**, often found together with **2**. Many were produced in the USA by Stevens-Savage Arms Company and were marked with either version of **15**. Those used in India were usually stamped with the India Government mark **9**, though **10**—India Stores—was used on the distinct India Patterns.

American bayonet makers' marks

AERIAL	Aerial Cutlery Company, Chicago and New York City
A F H	Allied Fork & Hoe Company, Geneva, Ohio
A C CO, A C C	American Cutlery Company, Marinette, Wisconsin
B M CO	Beckwith Manufacturing Corporation
	H Boker & Company, New York City
CAMILLUS, CAMCO	Camillus Cutlery Company, Camillus, New York
	W R Case & Sons Cutlery Company, Bradford, Pennsylvania
COLLINS, LEGITIMUS	Collins & Company, Hartford and Colinsville, Connecticut
COLONIAL	Colonial Cutlery Company, Providence, Rhode Island
	Colt's Patent Firearms Manufacturing Company (now Firearms Division of Colt's Industries), Hartford, Connecticut
MILPAR	Columbus & Milpar Manufacturing Company, Columbus, Ohio
HDS, HD & S	Henry Disston & Son, Philadelphia, Pennsylvania
GENEVA FORGE	Ecko Products Company, Chicago, Illinois
IMPERIAL, I C C	Imperial Cutlery Company, Providence, Rhode Island
J & D	Jones & Dickson Tool Company (?)
KINFOLKS, K I	Kinfolks Incorporated, Little Valley, New York
LF & C, L & C (?)	Landers, Frary & Clark, New Britain, Connecticut
O C L, O L (?)	Oneida Community Limited, Oneida, New York
PAL	Pal Blade & Tool Company, Plattsburg, New York
	Fayette R Plumb, Chicago and St Louis
R C C, R C CO	Robeson Cutlery Company, Perry, New York
R I A	Rock Island Arsenal, Rock Island, Illinois
S A	Springfield Armory, Springfield, Massachusetts
T M N	Turner Manufacturing Company, Statesville, New York
ULSTER	Ulster Knife Company, Walden, New York
U F H	United Fork & Hoe Company (?), Grand Rapids, Michigan
U, UNION	Union Cutlery Company, Olean, New York
UTICA, U C C, KA-BAR	Utica Cutlery Company, Utica, New York
V P Co	Victory Plastics Company
WESTERN	Western Cutlery Company, Boulder, Colorado

1   2   3   4   5   6   7   8   9   10   11   12

13   14   15

German bayonet makers' marks

This listing is far from comprehensive, and only charts the most important of the cutlery firms who are known to have manufactured, finished or retailed bayonets. Those marked with an asterisk (*) are thought to have been either finishers of partly-complete weapons or merely retailers. Further information can be found in *The sword and bayonet makers of Imperial Germany 1871-1918* by John Walter. The dates given below are those between which the firms are thought to have made bayonets, and are not those in which they worked.

crown/AMBERG	Amberg Gewehrfabrik, Amberg	1871-1918
	Anker-Werke*, Bielefeld	1914-1918
	Hugo Baruch & Co*, Berlin	1910-1918
	J H Becker & Co, Solingen	1914-1918
bow-and-arrow	J E Bleckmann, Solingen	1860-1918
football	Böntgen & Sabin 'Bönsawerke', Solingen	1914-1918
standing knight	W Clauberg & Co, Solingen	1870-1918
scales, ALCOSO	Alexander Coppel GmbH & Co, Solingen	1860-1945
script 'C'	Coulaux Frères, Klingenthal, Alsace	1870-1880
	J Corts Sohn, Remscheid	1914-1945
crown/DANZIG	Danzig Gewehrfabrik, Danzig	1914-1918
DEMAG	Deutsche Maschinenfabrik, Duisburg	1914-1918
	L O Dietrich*, Altenburg in Thüringen	1914-1945
script 'D'	Dürkopp-Werke AG, Bielefeld	1914-1945
squirrel, ORIGINAL	Carl Eickhorn, Soligen	1900-1945
crown/ERFURT	Erfurt Gewehrfabrik, Erfurt	1870-1918
horse on mound	Ferdinand Esser & Co, Elberfeld	1914-1945
	Fichtel & Sachs*, Schweinfurt	1914-1918
	Frister & Rossmann*, Berlin	1914-1918
	Carl Galle & Co*, Solingen	1914-1918
	Carl Grah & Co*, Solingen	1914-1918
	C G Haenel Waffen- und Fahrradfabrik, Suhl	1880-1945
pyramid, NIROSTA	Gottlieb Hammesfahr, Solingen-Foche	1914-1945
	Gebrüder Heller, Marienthal im Harz(?)	1914-1945
twins	J A Henckels 'Zwillingswerk', Solingen	1880-1945
crossed keys	Friedrich A Herder & Sohn, Solingen	1914-1945
four-point star	Richard A Herder, Solingen	1914-1918
	Friedrich A Hermes, Solingen	1875-1885
thermometer	F W Höller, Solingen	1900-1945
H,S, sword monogram	E & F Hörster, Solingen	1880-1945
crossed swords, C K	Carl Kaiser & Co, Solingen	1880-1900
	Heinrich Kaufmann 'Indiawerk', Solingen	1914-1918
knight's helm	W R Kirschbaum, Solingen	1860-1883
	E Knecht, Solingen	1914-1918
elephant's head	F Koeller, Solingen-Ohligs	1914-1945
	P D Lüneschloss, Solingen	1875-1918
	Waffenfabrik Mauser AG, Oberndorf am Neckar	1914-1918

	Johann Mehlich AG, Berlin	1914-1918
	J Mundlos & Co*, Magdeburg	1914-1945
	M & N Neumann*, Berlin	1910-1918
	Odeon-Werke Suhl (?)	1914-1918
blacksmith	Ernst Pack & Söhne*, Solingen	1910-1945
	Pack, Ohliger & Co, Solingen	1914-1945
knight/BAYARD	Anciens Établissements Pieper, Herstal	1914-1916
RØM	Rheinische Metallwaren-und Maschinenfabrik	
	(RM & M, later Rheinmetall-Borsig), Sömmerda	1898-1902
	Samson-Werke, Suhl	1914-1918
	V C Schilling, Suhl	1885-1915
trumpeting angel	Ferdinand Schleutermann, Remscheid-Hasten	1914-1945
	Schubert & Salzer*, Chemnitz	1914-1945
	A W Schulte & Co*, Gevelsberg	1914-1918
	E Siepmann & Co, Solingen	1914-1918
	Simson & Co (formerly Gebrüder Simson), Suhl	1875-1915
crown/SPANDAU	Spandau Gewehrfabrik, Spandau	1914-1945
	Richard Stock & Co, Berlin-Marienfelde	1914-1945
	Walter & Co*, Mühlhausen in Thüringen	1914-1945
king's head	Gebrüder Weyersberg (1), Solingen	1860-1883
trumpet	Gebrüder Weyersberg (2), Solingen-Wald	1935-1945
	Paul Weyersberg, Solingen	1935-1945
knight's helm	Weyersberg, Kirschbaum & Co, Solingen	1883-1920
king's head	WKC Stahl-und Eisenwarenfabrik, Solingen	1920-1945
W & ST	Weyersberg & Stamm, Solingen	1855-1870
	Ernst Wilhelm, Suhl	1870-1880
	Anton Wingen Jr, Solingen	1914-1945